How to Influence
and Persuade

How to Influence and Persuade

2nd edition

Jo Owen

PEARSON

Harlow, England • London • New York • Boston • San Francisco • Toronto • Sydney
Auckland • Singapore • Hong Kong • Tokyo • Seoul • Taipei • New Delhi
Cape Town • São Paulo • Mexico City • Madrid • Amsterdam • Munich • Paris • Milan

PEARSON EDUCATION LIMITED

Edinburgh Gate
Harlow CM20 2JE
Tel: +44 (0)1279 623623
Fax: +44 (0)1279 431059
Website: www.pearson.com/uk

First published in Great Britain in 2010 as *How To Influence* (print)
Second edition published in 2012 as *How to Influence and Persuade* (print and electronic)

Pearson Education is not responsible for the content of third-party internet sites.

ISBN: 978-0-273-77679-6 (print)
      978-0-273-77844-8 (PDF)
      978-0-273-77843-1 (ePub)

British Library Cataloguing-in-Publication Data
A catalogue record for this book is available from the British Library

Library of Congress Cataloging-in-Publication Data
A catalog record for this book is available from the Library of Congress

10 9 8 7 6 5 4 3 2 1
16 15 14 13 12

Typeset in 10pt Plantin Regular by 30.
Printed and bound in Great Britain by Ashford Colour Press Ltd., Gosport

NOTE THAT ANY PAGE CROSS REFERENCES REFER TO THE PRINT EDITION

Contents

Influence and persuade: the skills index   vii

Introduction   ix

Part 1   The ten pillars of influence   **1**

1   Whispers of influence: the persuasive
conversation   3

2   Active listening: two ears and one mouth   29

3   Earning the currency of influence: trust   41

4   Act the part   61

5   Win–win–win   79

6   Give to take   97

7   Play the right tune   111

8   The spider's web: building incremental
commitment   135

9   Build your platform   165

10   Turning dreams into reality   181

Part 2   Influence in practice   **199**

11   Moments of truth   201

12   The myths and reality of influence   223

Index   255

Influence and persuade: the skills index

1. Persuade people to agree   6
2. Ask smart questions   13
3. Presenting your idea   18
4. Overcoming objections   20
5. Listening to gain support   31
6. Make people talk   32
7. Paraphrase for clarity   35
8. Contradict for compliance   36
9. Build trust   44
10. Build personal credibility   48
11. Turn risk to your advantage   51
12. Act the part   64
13. Look the part   66
14. Speak the part   68
15. Use eye contact   72
16. Make great first impressions   73
17. Network effectively   74
18. Create a win–win   82
19. Move from positions to interests   84
20. Open negotiating options   87
21. Craft a story which sells   90
22. Focus your generosity   104
23. Ensure your generosity is valued   106
24. Understand people's self image   117
25. Understand your own style   124
26. Adapt your style when needed   125

27. Getting an introduction   139
28. Writing letters which work   140
29. Build commitment   145
30. Use territory well   148
31. Put recognition to work   149
32. Gain commitment by ceding control   154
33. Building a bandwagon   158
34. Dealing with conflict in private   159
35. Borrowing credibility and influence   167
36. Finding the sources of power   171
37. Staking your claim to fame   175
38. Control your agenda   177
39. Finding a great idea   185
40. Building a great team   188
41. Managing money challenges   191
42. Turning crises into opportunities   194
43. Finding the right assignment   204
44. Taking control   208
45. Negotiating budgets   211
46. Influencing decisions   212
47. Making meetings work   215
48. Presenting well   217
49. Handling conflict   220
50. Flatter to succeed   229

Introduction

I was Mr Zest and in the next cubicle sat Mr Fairy. I was responsible for Zest (a toilet soap). He was responsible for a competitor: Fairy Toilet Soap. On balance, I preferred to be Mr Zest than Mr Fairy. Suddenly, the CEO appeared by our cubicles: he was on walkabout. He asked me how things were going. I muttered something about the weather. He moved on to Mr Fairy and asked the same question.

'Jurgen,' said Mr Fairy, 'I would really like your advice on this new promotion we are developing...' The CEO was delighted. He had started his career in marketing. This was his chance to show that he had lost none of his marketing skills. Fifteen minutes later Jurgen left with a big smile on his face: he had just proven he still had the right stuff. Mr Fairy also had a big smile. He had just got the CEO's support for a controversial new promotion, and had made his name with the big boss. Word quickly spread that the Fairy project was now the CEO's pet project. One week later, all the staff departments had waved Fairy's promotion through. One month later, I was still battling with them to gain approval for my far more modest promotion.

It was a classic influencing moment, when power visibly shifts from one person to another. For many years, I was baffled by how some people seemed to ooze influence and get their way effortlessly. Meanwhile, others toil away and achieve far less. Slowly, I found that these moments were not random. There are consistent patterns of success and failure.

In that short exchange with the CEO, Mr Fairy had demonstrated several key influencing techniques:

- He seized the moment.
- He sold his idea by asking for advice: he listened rather than pitching.
- He had acted as a partner to the boss, treating him as a human not just a boss.
- He borrowed the authority of the CEO.

Eventually, I identified ten core skills that all good influencers have. And the good news is that anyone can learn them and become more influential. The result is that you can achieve far more with far less. Influence and persuasion are not 'nice to have' skills. They are 'must have' skills. Managing by command and control is dying. You can no longer just tell people what to do. The days of deference are over. To make things happen, you cannot do it all yourself. There are only 24 hours in a day. You have to enlist the support of colleagues and friends to achieve your dreams. But they have their own dreams and deadlines to think about as well: so how do you gain their support for your needs?

In the past, the job of managers was to make things happen through people they controlled. Managers still have to make things happen through other people, but they no longer control the people they rely on. Influence and persuasion are the core skills of management today.

influence and persuasion are the core skills of management today

Research is useless unless it can be put into practice. Over the last ten years I have been putting the principles of influence into practice, to see if they really work. And they have worked better than I ever dared to dream. If I had been told ten years ago that influence would have let me achieve the following, I would have said it was impossible:

- Setting up six national charities. One, Teach First, is set to be the largest graduate recruiter in the UK by 2013.

- Helping over 250 ex-offenders set up their own, legitimate, businesses. Only one in 25 have re-offended: nationally, two out of three ex-offenders normally land up in prison again.

- Creating a bank, which went on to become HBOS business banking.

- Building a business in Japan over three years, without speaking Japanese.

And when I started I knew nothing about education; I knew nothing about graduate recruitment; I knew nothing about offenders and the justice system. And I certainly knew nothing about banking: some people might argue that the credit crunch shows that top bankers did not know anything about banking either.

All of these things have been achieved with and through other great people. Alone, these dreams would have remained impossible dreams. But with influence and persuasion you can turn your dreams into reality. Because influence means working with others, it means you share the burden. You achieve more, work less.

Influence versus persuasion

This book covers both influence and persuasion. Persuasion is important, but dangerous. If you persuade someone the wrong way, you lose influence. We have all been victims of sales people, colleagues or bosses who use brilliant persuasion techniques to make us do something we later regret. And next time we see that person, we know not to trust them. They can use the tricks of persuasion to fool us once, but we will not be fooled again. This book shows how you can persuade and build influence at the same time: instead of avoiding you, people will want to work with you more. But you must persuade them the right way.

Influencers play for much higher stakes than persuaders. Influencers do not want a one-off success. They want to build commitment which lasts. This means that influencers think and act very differently from persuaders. Persuaders start and finish with their own needs. They want to sell their product or plant their idea in another person's head. Communication tends to be one way: the persuader does most of the talking as he or she extols the virtues of the product or idea they want to push.

Influencers still have goals to achieve, but think differently about how to get there. They see the world through other people's eyes, and adapt their message and behaviour accordingly. The ideal outcome is not simply to persuade someone: it is to build an alliance of mutual trust and respect. Achieving this is a huge investment of time, effort and skill. But it is an investment which yields rich dividends over a long period.

The differences between influence and persuasion are summarised in the table below:

Persuasion	Influence
Transaction	Relationship
Win–lose	Win–win
Competitive	Collaborative
One-off event	Permanent
Zero sum game	One plus one equals two
Short-term goals	Long-term goals
Me versus you	We
See my own needs only	See each others' needs
Kills trust	Builds trust

Persuasion is the here and now skill we have to learn. Influence is our investment in the future. If you think you are going to have to deal with someone regularly, it pays to learn influence and persuasion. If you think you will never meet someone again, then you can use every trick in the persuader's little black book: you need not worry about what that will do to your influence and trust.

Learning to influence and persuade

This is not a cook book. There is no secret recipe which allows you to create a magic potion called influence and persuasion. Instead, you can learn a range of skills and techniques. You do not have to learn them all at once. Try one skill at a time. Each skill will make you a better influencer and a better persuader. Learn all of them, and you will acquire a sort of magic in which people appear to be willing to follow you.

This book is not written with the idea that you start at page one and then you become a brilliant influencer by the time you finish reading the final page. Real life is not like that. We learn from experience more than anything else. So this is a guide to the skills you can and should start experimenting with. Feel free to switch between chapters. Each chapter is written so that it can be read as a stand alone skill: you do not have to have read every previous chapter to make sense of the skill. There is no grand unifying theory behind the book: this book is not a PhD thesis. It is for practising managers who need to cope with the daily reality of dealing with difficult colleagues, customers and bosses.

Each skill is the product of constant trial and error. I illustrate both the failures and successes. The failures are important: if you can avoid the many pitfalls I fell into in the course of working on this book, then that will save you considerable pain. Each of the skills is illustrated with real life examples. The good news is that you do not have to follow a script to be influential or persuasive. You can be yourself with your own unique style. But behind that style is a rigorous set of skills, structures and ways of thinking which enable you to succeed.

The mindset of influence

Influence is invisible because it is about how people think. We can not see people's thoughts. Thoughts drive behaviour which drives actions and results. We can look at the results that influential people achieve but still have no idea about what makes them influential. Just as we can not understand a person by looking at his shadow, we can not understand influence by looking at its effect. We have to look for the causes of influence, not at its symptoms.

Over 60 skills and principles of influence are outlined in this book. Behind those skills lie four ways of thinking which separate effective influencers from the rest of us. Thinking like an influencer is the first and most important step to becoming an influencer. We can use and adapt these four principles to suit our own style. We do not need to sell our soul or clone our brain to become influential. We do not need to become someone else. We simply need to build on the best of who we already are.

The four ways of influential thinking are:

1 Be ambitious.
2 Walk in other people's shoes.
3 Build commitment.
4 Start at the end.

1 Be ambitious

Lack of ambition is a recipe for a quiet life in the backwaters of under-achievement. For many people, the greatest barrier to success is in their heads. They accept low expectations for themselves. Low expectations are always self-fulfilling. Ambitious people have high expectations of themselves and others. They reach for the stars. Even if they fail and only reach the moon, they will be far ahead of others whose expectations reach no further than next year's

> the world has never been changed by unambitious people

beach vacation. The world has never been changed by unambitious people. Ambitious people are not satisfied with the status quo. They want to change things and make things happen.

Ambition which is all 'me...me...me' is not influential. It leads to conflict and fails to build networks of trust and support. Ambition which is 'we...we...we' is influential. It stretches people and teams, and builds commitment and camaraderie. The mindset of ambition is both positive and opportunity focused.

Ambition can make influential people uncomfortable to work with. They can be driven, focused and intense in a way that less influential people find intimidating. They often appear to be unreasonable: they will stretch people and ask them to do more than they thought possible. Stretching people can build, not wreck, relationships. When people are stretched, they grow and develop and are proud of what they have achieved. That builds loyalty to the person that led them to exceed their own expectations. Stretch is ineffective when it leads to stress, not pressure. The great dividing line between stress and pressure is control: people under pressure who still have control over their fate can perform exceptionally well. People under pressure who have no control over events quickly discover stress and burnout.

2 Walk in other people's shoes

We all like to think we are the centre of the universe. Influencers may also think that they are the centre of the universe, but they do not always show it. They work hard to see the world through the eyes of each person they want to influence. They are always asking themselves difficult questions:

- Why should this person want to talk to me?
- Why should they want to follow or support me?
- What do they want, what do they not want – how can I use that to my advantage?

- How can I find out more about this person?
- What other choices do they have, why should they prefer my way?

Walking in other people's shoes is not about being nice to other people, or even agreeing with them. It is about understanding them. Once we understand someone we can start to play their tune.

The core skill for walking in other people's shoes is very simple: listen actively. Good influencers have two ears and one mouth, and use them in that proportion. We can only understand other people if we listen to them. Given that most people enjoy talking about their favourite subject, themselves, the simple act of listening builds rapport at the same time as building our knowledge of the people we want to influence.

3 Build commitment

The commitment mindset is central to the world of influence, not control. The control mindset likes hierarchy: power comes from position. This makes it very limiting: the control mindset does not reach beyond the barriers of the hierarchy to make things happen outside a limited range of control. The controlling mindset is enabled by the organisation, but also limited by it. The controlling mindset thinks that commitment is a one-way street: anyone lower in the organisation must show commitment to people higher in the organisation. Team work for a controlling manager means 'My way or no way': if you do not obey then you are not a good team player.

The commitment mindset is not constrained by hierarchy or by the formal limitations of power. The commitment mindset builds a network of informal alliances which enables the influencer to achieve things far beyond the dreams of the controlling mindset. Commitment is a two-way street based on mutual obligations. Building commitment takes time and skill. Influencers do not expect to build trusted partnerships overnight. These things take time. But once built, such partnerships can pay dividends for a lifetime.

There is a hard edge to the commitment mindset. The influencer may be generous, reliable, committed and adaptable in the quest to build trusted partnerships. But the influencer always expects something in return, and sets that expectation from the start of the relationship. Partnership means give and take. Bowing to the wishes of other people is the road to popularity and to weakness. Influencers learn that trust and respect are more valuable currencies than popularity.

> trust and respect are more valuable currencies than popularity

4 Start at the end

There is an old tale of a traveller who is lost in Ireland. He asks a local for directions to Dublin and is told: 'If I was going to Dublin... I wouldn't start from here.' We are where we are and we have to make the most of it. But from this truism comes another which grannies and gurus trot out at regular intervals: 'First things first.' This is a catastrophic piece of advice. It implies we start with what we have and proceed from there.

Instead of starting with what they have, influential people start at the end. They work out the desired goal and then work back from there. They map the journey from the destination back to today. If we start from where we are, we may decide that our goal (Dublin or any other goal) is not achievable. If we start at the end, the only question we should ask is 'how do we get there?' not 'can we get there?'

Starting at the end is a mindset which consistently drives different and more effective behaviour. It is focused on the future not the past; on action not analysis; and on outcomes not on process. The mindset shows itself in the questions asked in common day-to-day situations:

- Crises: 'how do we move forward?' not 'what went wrong and who can I blame?'
- Conflicts: 'what are we arguing about and is it worth it?' not 'how do I win?'
- Meetings: 'what will we achieve in this meeting?' not 'what is the formal agenda?'
- Project planning: 'what is our goal?' not 'what is the process and where is the risk log?'
- Presentations: 'what is my key message and for who?' not 'can we prepare another 50 PowerPoint slides, just in case we get a question?'

Starting at the end requires firmness about the goals but flexibility about the means. This flexibility makes it much easier to adapt to other people and to build commitment. People who are stuck in the control way of thinking lack such flexibility: they hope that strict compliance with a process will yield the right outcome. They use the same map, whatever their journey may be. However hard they run, they never make progress: they simply cover the same course faster. Starting at the end ensures the influencer chooses a worthwhile destination. They may not always travel the fastest, but at least they make progress.

Part 1

The ten pillars of influence

Chapter 1

Whispers of influence: the persuasive conversation

The dark arts of persuasion cover many sins: bribery, blackmail, bullying, deceit, deception, cold calling and plain persistence can all work. Attractive and effective as many of these tools may seem, we will set them to one side. None of them are needed for you to be persuasive. There is a subtler art of persuasion which all managers eventually must learn if they are to succeed. This is the art of the persuasive conversation: convincing others to support you and your ideas. Do this well and they will follow you willingly, not reluctantly. It is like magic to control such conversations and persuade colleagues to support you.

A persuasive conversation is not a random conversation. Social conversations can meander, and that is a large part of their pleasure. A persuasive conversation has a structure and a purpose. *Every* persuasive conversation has the same structure. You can use the same structure whether you are engaged in a two-minute conversation or a two-year conversation about some big new initiative. The beauty of the structure is that it is both invisible and flexible. Only you will know that you are using the structure. And it is flexible enough that you will talk normally and naturally. You will not sound like one of those hapless cold calling telesales people who are reading the same script time and again.

A persuasive conversation gains more than agreement: it also builds commitment. People will trust you more and want to work with you more. Effective persuasion builds your influence; ineffective persuasion destroys your influence. Many training courses and books focus on the wrong sort of persuasion, the sort where you trick or force people into agreement. You can pull the trick once, but next time you will meet a wall of resistance from the person you tricked.

All persuasive conversations have the same structure, although the conversation may last from two minutes to two years. It is a structure I learned when selling nappies in Birmingham. I have used it since to start a bank, sell consulting in Japan and persuade colleagues to lend their support. The context, goals, culture and timeframe change, but the structure does not.

The structure follows seven steps. Since I can never remember seven of anything, I have simplified it into an acronym: PASSION. Acronyms may be ugly, but they make it easier to remember each step. And to make it even easier, I think of each step as a set of traffic lights which are at red. I can not proceed to the next stage of the conversation until each set of lights has turned green. That gives time and breathing space to think about what comes next. Here are the seven steps of the PASSION principle:

1 **P**reparation
2 **A**lignment
3 **S**ituation review
4 **S**o what's in it for me ('WIFM')
5 **I**dea
6 **O**vercome objections and obstacles
7 **N**ext steps

To show how fast this structure can flow, let's look at a simplified example. The team had been working late and wanted to keep working. I thought they all needed a break if they were to be productive the next day: time to get them out of the office and down to the bar:

1 Preparation: make sure the whole team was in the room. Check with a couple of them that they were as tired as they looked. Ask for their attention.

2 Alignment: 'Its been a hard week, how are you all feeling?' Groans of tiredness and mutterings of discontent were all that came by way of reply.

3 Situation review: 'We're all tired. We need a break.'

4 So what's in it for me: 'We need to be fresh for the big push tomorrow, and a bit more team morale would not be bad either.'

5 Idea: 'Let's go to the bar around the corner.'

6 Overcome objections and obstacles: 'I'll buy the first round.'

7 Next steps: 'Last person out turns off the lights and buys the second round.'

That persuasive conversation lasted seconds before the stampede to the door started. Other conversations are not quite so easy, take more time and require more finesse.

Do not worry if the structure looks hard. Like learning to play a sport or a musical instrument, it takes time and practice. The more you use the structure, the better you will become. It will become second nature to you, and it will be invisible to the person you are persuading. But before embarking on the structure of the conversation, try working on some of the principles that lie behind the structure.

You can use any or all of these principles to become a more effective persuader. Try using just one principle to start with when you are persuading people. You will find the task of persuasion becomes easier with each principle you deploy. Equally, when things go wrong, I normally find it is because I have ignored one or more of these basic principles.

The ten principles of persuasion

1   The noddy principle: an effective conversation has your opposite number nodding in agreement from the start. You may start simply by agreeing that it is a rainy or sunny day. But start the agreement process early. If they say something you disagree with, do not object and start an argument. Ignore the comment. Focus on areas of agreement. The idea is to slowly funnel the discussion towards your desired outcome.

2   The listening principle. Great persuaders have two ears and one mouth, and use them in that proportion. They listen more than they talk. Let people talk themselves into agreement. The more they talk, the more you find out about how best to present your idea. Let people talk about their favourite subject: themselves.

3   Win–win principle: a win–lose discussion is a conflict. Identify how you can both win and you will have a much more productive conversation. Craft a story which allows the other person to show how smart they were.

4   The emotional engagement principle: it is easy to disagree with people you dislike, harder to argue against people you like. Get onto your counterpart's wavelength early. If they annoy you, do not show it. Wear the mask of friendship.

5   Other people's shoes principle: do not try to batter people into submission with the brilliance of your idea and logic. You will simply annoy them and give them material to argue about. See how it looks from their side: what's in it for them, why they might object and what you can do to prevent them objecting?

6   The options principle: have a best case outcome and be prepared to work backwards from it. But always have a Plan B. When you are sailing against the wind the quickest way forward is not a straight line: it is a zigzag. Learn to be flexible.

7   The partnership principle: you are neither telling someone, nor being told, what to do. You are working together to discover a good outcome. This is especially important when dealing with important people. If you act junior,

they will treat you as a junior. Treat them not as a boss, but as a human being and as your partner in developing an idea or action.

8   The positive principle: be positive both in style and in substance. If you are not positive and enthusiastic about your idea, don't expect anyone else to be positive and enthusiastic for you.

9   The traffic lights principle. Think of the conversation structure as a series of traffic lights which are at red. Do not proceed to the next stage until the lights turn green. Do not get ahead of yourself: take your time and make sure each step is complete before moving to the next.

10 Next steps principle. Always have some next steps at the end of every conversation, otherwise the trail goes cold. Do not assume the other person is psychic: they will not know what the next steps are, so you have to suggest next steps to them.

Each of these influencing and persuading principles are explored in more detail later in the book. If all you do is to apply some of these principles some of the time, you will find that you will become more persuasive and more influential.

Everyone has their own unique style and way of deploying the principles and structure of persuasion: it is not a mechanistic script which you have to read. To start with, focus on one step (preparing the conversation) and any one of the ten principles you feel most comfortable with. With practice you can build up more steps and more principles. By way of consolation, rest assured that even the most accomplished persuaders still mess up and are still learning after decades of experience. The goal is not perfection. The goal is improvement.

Persuasive conversations: the structure

Remember the hidden structure of the persuasive conversation has seven stages, or seven traffic lights which you must pass through:

1   **P**reparation

2   **A**lignment

3   **S**ituation review

4   **S**o what's in it for me ('WIFM')

5   **I**dea

6   **O**vercome objections and obstacles

7   **N**ext steps

The structure is the same in every situation. To illustrate it, I have taken a real case. My job was to persuade a potential client, who I had never met, that they should buy our services. I knew that they already had an outline agreement with McKinsey for the same work, and McKinsey shared the same building as the client. And the client was in Tokyo, so language was an interesting challenge. The structure was the same structure used to persuade colleagues to be more helpful, to persuade funders and government ministers to support charities I was setting up, to gain support of clients and colleagues as far apart as Saudi Arabia, Belgium and the United States. Whatever the context, the structure remains the same.

1 Preparation

time spent preparing is rarely wasted

Time spent preparing is rarely wasted. The preparation may take 15 seconds as you walk towards someone's office, or it may take days as you prepare for a big meeting. Your preparation checklist covers five basic questions:

- What do I want to achieve in this meeting?
  - What is my Plan B which takes me half way to the goal?
- How will the other person see this issue?
  - What are their no-go areas?
  - What are their hot buttons: what will turn them on?
  - Why would they want to support this idea?

- How should I interact with them? What is their style?
- Are any logistics required for the meeting: phones, conference numbers, flip charts, room layout, number of people, room bookings etc.
- How will I start the meeting?

For our first formal meeting with the Tokyo bank we spent several days doing our homework: finding out as much about the business as possible, who was going to be at the meeting and what, if anything, we knew about them. Having found out that the competition was McKinsey, we realised there was no point in going head to head with a smarty-pants presentation. We would have to change the rules of the game and have a more interactive and more participative meeting. We set this expectation, making it clear that it would be an example of the way we would run the project with them.

We also sent in advance a short summary of our relevant credentials: we did not want to waste time in the meeting boasting about ourselves. The more time you spend talking about yourself, the more likely you are to bore or annoy your client or colleague. We wanted to engage the client and make them start talking instead of hearing us pitch and judging us. Good persuaders learn to be self-effacing: the opposite of the charismatic extrovert who tries to talk everyone into surrender.

Although we were going to have a discussion, not a presentation, the preparation was intense. Preparing for a discussion is much harder than preparing for a presentation. A presentation runs on a fixed path. A discussion can go in many directions, depending on the reactions you get. We had to prepare for all the different ways in which the discussion could go, and we very tightly scripted the outcome we actually wanted.

2 Alignment

This is where you need to start walking in the other person's shoes. You need to help them answer some questions which they will have in their heads:

● What is this discussion all about?
● Why should I talk to this person about this subject?
● Am I prepared to believe this person?
● Why am I talking now?

This part of the discussion starts socially and finishes professionally. The better you know someone, the quicker alignment can happen. It can be as fast as 'Hi Sam, how are you?' If Sam looks grumpy and harassed, it may be worth seeing what is chewing him up: if it is a bad time to talk, let Sam sort his problems out and fix another time to meet.

At first meetings, alignment takes time and effort. They will be keen to know who you are and, bluntly, if it is worth talking to you. Making a formal pitch about your credentials may be necessary, but can backfire. They may be unimpressed, or they may dislike your boasting. Either way, it puts you in the position of a supplicant and them in the position of judge and jury: it is not a partnership discussion. The better way of doing this is to find some common background: places you have worked, people you both know, conferences attended. These professional links are a chance to show that you know what you are talking about. Do not get into a bragging contest about who has the best experience. Use the opportunity to flatter and soothe an executive ego: be suitably impressed by what they claim to have achieved and the challenges they have faced. Even areas of social overlap such as pastimes build some mutual respect.

Once the other side is comfortable that they are talking to the right person at the right time, you can move explicitly to the main subject of discussion.

When we got to the bank the meeting started with the formal exchange of *meishi* (business cards). We quickly found we had many areas of common background and experience: we had identified some areas from our research. They had identified some areas from our advance materials. It was a social chat which confirmed to them that we might know what we were talking about. Once they were relaxed we outlined how we wanted to run the meeting: we laid out an agenda and objective which demanded that they participate rather than us present. This was the expectation that we had set, and they were happy to humour us. We made no presentation at all.

3 Situation review

If you can both agree on the problem or opportunity, the chances are that the solution will be relatively easy to find. In many cases, persuasive conversations go wrong because the two sides have different views about what the problem or opportunity is. Invest time to agree the problem explicitly. Even if you both agree the problem in broad outline, the chances are that you will have different perspectives on it. Explore these perspectives. You do not need to persuade at this moment: you need to listen.

Remember to focus on their issue, opportunity or problem, not on yours. Understand how they see the world before you try changing their view of the world. It is better to ask smart questions, than to make smart comments. Smart questions are ones which get rich answers. Dumb questions get yes/no answers. Even if you get lucky with a 'yes' you have not learned anything about why they said yes. And if they say no, you hit a dead end. The smart/dumb comments are just that. They may be very smart and based on deep insight and knowledge. But they are also dumb because they invite a pointless argument.

> it is better to ask smart questions, than to make smart comments

Smart questions	Dumb questions	Smart/dumb comments
What are your priorities for the next year?	Is x your priority for the next year	Our analysis shows that x, y and z are your top priorities
How do your clients see this?	Do your clients like this?	Our research shows that your clients will love this
What do you see as the major obstacles to progress?	Is this a major obstacle to success?	I know this looks like a real obstacle, but it is not
Why is this important to you?	Is this important to you?	Of course, everyone accepts that this is important and urgent

If the conversation later on goes wrong, come back to this point: reaffirm what it is that you are trying to accomplish together. Step 3 is the logical choke point of the conversation. If in doubt, always come back to this point to clarify and confirm.

In the case of the Tokyo bank, this was the critical step. We had to reframe the problem for them. They had framed the problem as cutting costs. We knew this was unlikely: banking was growing, and firing people in Japan is as close as you can get to corporate suicide. So we got the bank to talk about their business. They proudly told us it was growing. We chatted about how one western firm had reneged on some employment offers: they agreed that such employment practices would be a disaster for them. Slowly we let them discover that they did not want to cut total costs: they wanted to keep costs steady while trading volumes rose. This was a radical reformulation of the problem leading to radically different solutions. As soon as we had made this breakthrough with them, we were winning. Simply by helping them reframe the problem, we had added huge amounts of credibility and value to them. And we had not shown them any paper or made any presentations: we had simply chatted. But it was a very structured and purposeful chat.

Once you have agreed the nature of the problem or the opportunity, the traffic lights should turn green in your mind and you can proceed to the next stage of the conversation.

4 So what's in it for me? ('WIFM')

Now a huge bear trap opens up. It is tempting to leap to the solution and discuss how it works. If you do this, you will be speeding through several sets of red traffic lights. You may get lucky and survive, but you may well crash and burn. Take it easy. You are slowly building commitment; keep them nodding, keep them on your side.

Before they agree with your brilliant idea, they will have two questions rattling in the back of their mind:

- What are the benefits of your idea to me personally, and to my organisation?
- What are the risks to me personally, and to my organisation?

Your first task is to explore the benefits of your idea. Leave the risks and problems until later. People buy solutions, not problems. If you focus on the problems too early, you will depress and discourage everyone and they will give up. They need the motivation of knowing what's in it for them and their organisation.

Benefits are rational, emotional and political. We normally focus on the rational benefits only, but humans are not computers. We have emotions. As social animals we also have politics. Be aware of all the benefits and risks of your idea.

Rational benefits are obvious. Some are financial: save money, make more profit. Many non-financial benefits also have financial implications: reducing time to market; reducing the amount of re-offending by prisoners; getting unemployed people into work; improving quality and reducing warranty claims. Establish the financial impact of all of these benefits. Size the prize. If you are able to dangle a carrot worth millions in front of someone, then most people will start to show interest. The art is not to tell them 'this is worth millions': that invites argument. Discuss it with them, produce the estimate together. If it is their estimate, they will believe it.

Political benefits and risks come down to a simple question: 'How will this affect me in my organisation?' No one wants to be the village idiot who backed a dumb idea or made a bad decision or negotiated poorly. You need to approach these issues crabwise: from the side. Diving overtly into the politics of your organisation and your partner is unlikely to be productive. Instead, you can ask smart questions to reveal what the political landscape looks like:

> no one wants to be the village idiot who backed a dumb idea

- Who else needs to buy in to this idea?
- How will they see this idea? What will they like about it? What risks will they see?
- How would you advise that we handle this issue when we see them?

When you frame the question this way, you give the other side the chance to air their personal fears under the guise of pretending that they are fears their colleagues have. Live with the deceit: it is a useful way of finding out what they really think.

Finally, you need to deal with the emotional aspects of your idea, which again come down to a simple question: 'what's in it for me?' This is the 'WIFM' question. Once you understand WIFM (or 'wiffim' as it is often called) for each person you are dealing with, you are on the high road to success. Or at least you will understand the real obstacles that lie on the road ahead.

The answer to WIFM may be positive: I will have more interesting work, better chances of promotion, look good in front of the boss, have less work, a problem will go away.

It may also be negative: I will have to work harder, it exposes me to risk of failure, it creates uncertainty, I will land up with a new boss, I simply do not understand how it might affect me.

The problem with emotional objections is that no one talks about them. They disguise them with rational concerns such as 'that is too risky, it will cost too much, health and safety will not allow it'. And the more you argue about these rational objections, the more you ignore their real objection. Things get ugly fast.

Most WIFM objections come down to perceived risk in terms of success, workload, reputation and so on. The key is to understand that risk is not absolute: it is relative. The default position of most people when faced with a risky idea is to kill it: doing nothing is less risky than doing something. So you have to change the balance of risk:

- Provide reassurance that the risks of your idea are modest and manageable.
- Show that the risks of doing nothing are real. Create the burning platform, find the bogeyman that will eat them up if they stand still.

All of this takes time. Don't rush. Ask smart questions which lead them to the answer you want them to discover.

For the Tokyo bank this was a simple step. We had already reframed the problem: it was not about cutting absolute costs, but keeping costs stable during growth. All we had to do now was to size the prize: how much growth did they expect at zero cost increase over how long? We did not tell them: we let them discuss and agree this. Having framed the desired outcome, we got them to put a value on the outcome. When they estimated the annual benefits at over $8 million a year, they started to reframe their own expectations about the scale of the project. They did not need a little advice; they needed serious support to drive major profit improvement. They successfully sold themselves a larger engagement.

We also worked on the rational and political challenges. In preparing for our meeting we had insisted that everyone who had responsibility for the programme had to be in the meeting. All the power barons were there. So if they made a dumb decision and hired us, at least they would all be dumb together. An iron rule of all organisations is that it is far better to be collectively wrong than to be individually right. If you are collectively wrong, then no one takes all the blame. If you are right and everyone else is wrong, you will find yourself isolated and the organisation will quickly re-write reality to show either that everyone else thought of your idea first, or that your idea is wrong.

Finally, we dealt with their emotional fears: cutting costs as originally proposed by them would have led to horrendous headlines in the media. We gave them an alternative: reduce unit costs through growth. We had removed all the risk for them.

5 Idea

By this point, you are 90% of the way to success. Your client or colleague is ready to say 'yes'. And yet you still have not actually proposed your idea. But your client and colleague now actively wants to hear your solution: they agree the problem, they see that there are big benefits in solving it and any risks or objections are known and manageable. So all they want to know is 'how'. At last, you are ready to tell them and they are ready to agree.

You have three ways of outlining your proposed idea.

Method one

The simplest way is to tell them, in one sentence: 'Let's start with an eight week assessment with a small team, which will then lead to a focused effort over nine months to deliver the results you want.'

You then move promptly to stage six (below) where you pre-empt and resolve any outstanding concerns they may have.

Method two

Offer them a choice, so that they feel ownership over the course of action that they pick. Naturally, you will have a preferred solution and so you will want to make sure they pick the right one.

If you offer a choice you change the terms of debate: you are no longer saying 'my way or no way'. You set up a partnership discussion in which you are finding the best solution together. The simplest version of this is the three choice trick:

- Choice A: very big and exciting, but you know is going to be too much and too risky.
- Choice B: this is the choice you prefer.
- Choice C: low risk, low effort but really does not get anyone anywhere.

Let the other person tell you in no uncertain terms why A and C are useless choices. Let them confirm to themselves their wisdom, business judgement and superiority. You can then profess your great thanks to them for guiding you to Choice B, which you wanted all along.

Method three

Ask your client or colleague to design the solution for you. In practice, you have to take them through a process of discovery so that they reveal to themselves the solution you have always wanted. This is more elaborate than the first two methods, but it is also more powerful. By letting someone come up with their own solution, you guarantee that they are genuinely committed to it. They can show off to others about how smart they were in figuring out the solution. Let them brag.

Being gluttons for punishment, this is the approach we took with our bank in Tokyo: we needed to make sure they were totally committed to our solution, so we had to help them discover it for themselves. This was not a random conversation: it was structured and directed. We asked the client to complete a project logic with us in the meeting. The project logic had four elements, in order:

1   Desired outcomes (one or two key goals). In their case it was growth at no cost while maintaining or improving quality.

2   Key success factors: to achieve this outcome, what needs to be in place? (eg effective IT systems, clear processes, revamped skills, measures and rewards and more besides).

3   So where would we need to be in two months' time if we have made a good start? This is where they designed the project start with us.

4   What do we need to do now to set the project up for success? This was our guide to managing the decision making process and politics.

By now the client had not only agreed to a project logic, but they had also emotionally committed to the project. It was their project, not just a consultant's project.

6 Overcome objections and obstacles: the art of persuasion judo

The best way to deal with problems and objections is to pre-empt them. If you have done your listening well in the early stages, you will know what the objections are likely to be, and you will be able to defuse them. For instance, if you know budget will be an objection, you might mention in advance that Finance have already looked at your idea. Even if they have not approved the idea, you can say that you are working with them to solve the problem.

Inevitably, there will be some objections. This is the 'yes but...' part of the conversation. People start to say things like 'yes, but have you thought of...' or 'I agree, but how about...'. Remember that everything before 'but' is baloney. They are raising their anxieties and concerns. There are many ways of dealing with

argument simply generates more argument

these concerns. Probably the worst way is to argue your case: the smarter you are, the more you will drive the other person into a corner. Argument simply generates more argument.

It is natural for us to react defensively to these objections: people are saying that they do not like our baby. The problem with a defensive reaction is that it simply provokes more argument. Soon enough both sides will be engaged in trench warfare to prove that they are right and the other side is wrong. The rational debate gets lost in the emotional need to be seen to be right.

So how can we defuse objections without fighting them? You use persuasion judo: use the force of their own argument to flatten their argument. There are three steps to persuasion judo:

Step one

Agree with the objection. This avoids the win/lose debate that results from a defensive reaction. The two of you are now in agreement (the noddy principle works again) and you face a common challenge. Here is the sort of language you can use:

- I agree...that has been worrying me.
- You're right...other people have been raising the same issue.

Step two

Outline a potential solution in a way which does not put you on the line for defending the idea. For instance:

'When I talked this through with other people, they came up with a range of solutions. One I liked in particular was...'

You have just depersonalised the disagreement. If the solution is no good, then the other person is no longer arguing with you: they are arguing with an absent third party who suggested the idea. You are both on safe ground still.

Step three

Ask for their advice. Ask if they have a better way of solving the challenge than the one you outlined. Again, the language can be simple:

'Of course, that was just one idea: would that work or do you have an even better way of dealing with it...'

So now you are getting your client or colleague to solve their own problem for you. Your judo throw is complete: problem solved without a fight.

And this is how we worked with the Bank: every problem they identified, they solved themselves. Every group has the potential to become competitive. Each person wants to outshine the next. This is dangerous, because each person may want to find ever greater risks and problems with your idea. You find yourself in a shooting gallery and you are the target. It isn't pretty. Persuasion judo turns the group dynamics on its head. Instead of each person competing to see who could find the biggest risk and obstacle, they were all competing to see who could find the smartest solution. They were doing our work for us.

7 Next steps

Never assume that you have agreement. Most managers are not great at telepathy. They will not know exactly what you want. Many people fall at this final hurdle. For instance, I was recently called in to see a government minister. I prepared thoroughly and it all went well. But I had been so focused on getting through the meeting that I had forgotten the most important thing of all: the close and the next steps. Government ministers have other things on their mind and do not have time to waste trying to work out what you are thinking or hoping for. You have to ask and be clear about what you want. Do not turn your golden opportunity into fool's gold.

> most managers are not great at telepathy

Confirm your agreement: what you think has happened may not be the same as what the other person thinks has happened. There are four main ways of closing the conversation. In the first three cases you get positive confirmation that you both understand what you have agreed:

- The direct close: 'So would you like to buy the car?' Very clear, but risky: you invite the answer no, in which case you get to start over again.

- The alternate close: 'Would you like to buy the silver car or blue car?' This is a sneaky close. You appear to be offering a choice, but you are not offering the choice of 'no'. Many people find it hard to resist this close.

- The action close: 'Here are the keys, I'll get the paperwork and as soon as you sign you can drive off.' This close has momentum built in which is hard to resist, and it is very clear.

- The assumed (confirmation) close: 'So we are all agreed that we will buy a fleet of pink and yellow striped mini-vans.' This is the sort of close used by chairmen at the end of meetings to summarise discussion. It takes a brave person to defy this close. But because it lacks positive confirmation from other people, there is a danger of this agreement unravelling later behind closed doors.

Once you have agreement, follow up. Fast. The longer you leave it, the more the agreement will go cold and second thoughts will start coming up. If possible, make the agreement public: once committed in public, people find it hard to back track. Send an email thanking them for their contribution and confirming the next steps: copy it to some relevant and interested parties. Ideally, give both parties a next step. You can show professionalism by following up. By asking for a next step from the other person you reinforce your mutual agreement and their commitment.

By the time we got to this stage, the Tokyo bank was ready to do the closing for us. One of the clients turned to us and asked: 'Have we just designed your project for you?'

'Yes,' I replied, 'Do you like it?'

'Of course!' said the client. They had done the selling for us. They had designed the project, so they owned it and were committed to it. We then quickly agreed next steps for moving ahead. As soon as we got back to the office we did not celebrate. We debriefed, followed up on our commitments. And then we celebrated.

Persuasive conversations: structural and emotional flow

The structure of your persuasive conversation is not just a rational framework. It is also an emotional framework in which you take someone on a journey from indifference or hostility to agreement and commitment. The traffic lights apply to each stage of the emotional journey as well as to the logic of your conversation. Here is how the structure of logic and emotion flow together. For the sake of simplicity I refer to the person you are persuading as a client, although they may be a colleague, supplier, regulator, vendor, partner or anyone else.

Conversation structure	Logical traffic lights	Emotional traffic lights
Preparation	You understand client, have objectives and have agreed logistics	Client accepts need for meeting; expectations set
Alignment	You have confirmed the purpose of the meeting	Client feels comfortable talking to you; credibility and rapport established
Situation review	You understand the situation from their perspective	Client is now relaxed and confident that they have been heard and understood

So what's in it for me?	You have established the 'size of the prize'	Client is excited by the potential win to the organisation and for self
Idea	You have stated your idea clearly and it is understood	Client confirms that they understand what you are asking for
Overcome objections and obstacles	Objections are understood, qualified and resolved	Client is on your side, working to resolve any problems
Next steps	You agree specific next steps with the client	Client expresses commitment to what happens next

The easiest way to see if the emotional traffic lights are green is to watch the body language. It is normally pretty obvious. If someone is leaning forward, smiling, talking warmly and positively you have green lights. If they are sitting back, arms folded, looking over your shoulder, looking at their smart phone, fidgeting and giving short and tetchy answers to you, it does not take a genius to work out that the emotional traffic lights are flashing bright red. When this happens, do not plough on. Go back to stages two and three: get some alignment and make sure you have understood what their perspective is.

By keeping this structure in your mind you can pace and direct the conversation as you see fit. You are not working to a script; you are not a pushy sales person. You are being yourself. But you have a structure which gives direction and purpose to your conversation. Your conversation becomes persuasive and productive.

Persuasion: the classic mistakes

Persuasive conversations rarely go wrong because the persuader has failed to master the esoteric art of the reverse flip flop bi-active power close. They go wrong because the basics go wrong. Here, from hard won experience, are some of the classics:

1   **Persuading the wrong person.** Do a brilliant job, gain agreement and find the person you are talking to is not the real decision maker. Solution: do your homework.

2   **Leaving without next steps.** This can happen even after a brilliant meeting where everything has gone well, but you forget to state exactly what happens next. It is then very awkward to go back a few days later and try to recreate the enthusiasm that existed before. And if things have not gone as planned, you always need a Plan B, which should at least involve a follow-up conversation. Solution: know the outcome you want, and ask for it.

3   **Falling in love with your own idea.** The result: you talk too much and talk over the other person who will not love your baby as much as you do. In fact, they may just see a noisy mess and will object to your baby. Listening is better than talking. Solution: ask smart questions, don't make smart comments. Failing that, buy duct tape and put it over your mouth.

4   **Becoming defensive.** When people object to your idea, it is easy to start arguing back. Then you just have an argument. It is better to win a friend than to win an argument. Solution: agree with the objection. Let them talk about their concerns. And use the WWF ('what we find') concept to tell them a non-threatening story which deals with their concern. Or, simply, ask them for advice on how they would solve their concern. Often they will solve their own problem.

5   **Not following up.** When you have an agreement, you need to reinforce it and confirm it. Otherwise, nothing will happen. Solution: send an email immediately after the meeting, thanking them for their great help and summarising the main conclusions and next steps.

6   **Having only a Plan A.** This is fine when things go well. But we have to deal with human nature. The unexpected happens. You need to prepare

for all eventualities, and to be flexible. Solution: have a Plan B: have an alternative outcome that you will accept. Your Plan A, B, C and Z should all have clear next steps.

7 **Hiding behind PowerPoint**. PowerPoint is a disaster for persuaders. It makes you talk, not listen. It gives you no flexibility. It puts the other person in the role of judge and jury: that is a role they will enjoy more than you, because you are the defendant they are judging. When was the last time you saw heads of government persuading each other at a summit with PowerPoint? Never. Solution: ditch PowerPoint.

Summary

The invisible structure behind the persuasive conversation has seven simple steps:

1 **P**reparation

2 **A**lignment

3 **S**ituation review

4 **S**o what's in it for me ('WIFM')

5 **I**dea

6 **O**vercome objections and obstacles

7 **N**ext steps

Apply this structure consistently and contentious discussions become cooperative, negative outcomes become positive and passive agreements become active support.

The persuasive conversation, like most influencing skills, is most effective when it is invisible. People should not feel that they are being persuaded or influenced. Gently guide them in the right direction. Let them discover the right answer. Done well, they will think it is their own idea. They will commit willingly and to the idea, whereas active persuading often leads to no more than passive and grudging agreement. Influencers go beyond that to build active and lasting support.

Chapter 2

Active listening: two ears and one mouth

What has listening got to do with influence? Listening may seem an odd place to start your influencing journey, not least because we all do plenty of listening anyway. So what more do we need to learn about listening?

Now turn things around. Who do you trust more: the person who tries to talk you into submission, or the person who takes time to listen to your needs and wants? There are plenty of people who have the gift of the gab; listening well is harder and more valuable. At the heart of good influencing is good listening. Great leaders, and influencers have two ears and one mouth, and use them in that proportion. They listen twice as much as they talk.

Good listening is effective for several reasons:

- You find out about the person who is talking: what matters to them, what they like and dislike, what they need. They are giving you the information you need to influence them effectively.

- People like talking about themselves, their job, their challenges.

- Listening builds trust and rapport: you appear to be on their side, as opposed to talkers who seem to follow their own agenda.

Good listening may be effective, but it is also an art form. You can not just sit down and hope that a stranger will start discussing their personal life with you. Strangers who do this are often well worth avoiding, especially on public transport. You need to know how to elicit the right information from the right people. Getting people to talk in a productive and purposeful manner is an art form.

Here are five principles to effective listening which we will explore in detail:

1 Open and purposeful questions.
2 Reinforcement: the coffee shop principle.
3 Paraphrasing.
4 Contradiction.
5 Disclosure.

1 Open and purposeful questions

When we first meet someone, it is very tempting to tell them who we are. It is human nature to puff ourselves up a little: we want to make a good impression and show that we are someone who is worth talking to. The problem with this approach is that it is boring. We may be a source of endless fascination to ourselves, but strangers really do not care. So turn this logic around. Ask the person you are meeting to talk about the most interesting subject on the planet: themselves. The simplest way to do this is to ask the Queen's question (she asks this question on walkabouts when meeting the great unwashed): 'what do you do...' There are more creative ways of asking the same question. Having studied tribes for years, I sometimes ask people what tribe they come from. Most people see their firm as a collection of tribes and dive straight into telling me all about their tribes and how they have to fight the other tribes and departments.

Once they have started talking, keep them talking. Do this by asking open, but directed questions.

An open question is one where it is impossible to reply yes/no: it encourages a rich answer. Open questions will often start 'How, what, why...' For instance:

- How does this work?
- What are the major risks/benefits of this?
- Why are they trying to stop this?

Each of these questions will encourage a rich reply. In contrast, closed questions invite a yes/no answer and may well kill off the discussion. The three open questions above can be posed as closed questions:

- Will this work?
- Is this worthwhile?
- Will they stop this?

These closed questions are very dangerous. The answer may not only be short: it may be the wrong answer. So if you ask 'will this work?' and the answer is 'no' you have a problem. Suddenly, the onus is on you to prove that it will work. But your colleague has already taken a position that it will not work. So now you are in an adversarial position and your colleague is not talking. You are not back at square one: you are in completely the wrong place if you want a productive conversation. If you ask 'how will this work' you get a much more useful reply. Perhaps the answer is 'it will only work with great difficulty and under these conditions...' but at least you have a constructive dialogue about how to make it work, rather than an argument about whether it will work.

Clearly, open questions are not random questions. There has to be purpose and direction behind your discussion. The art of the persuasive conversation was covered in detail in the last chapter. It is enough to make the point and illustrate it here. Take the question above:

- What are the major risks/benefits of this?

You have a choice: ask about the risks first or the benefits first. Your choice of order is likely to determine the success or otherwise of the conversation. If you ask for the risks first, you will get a very rich answer. People are normally risk averse and are very good at spotting risks. You will get a long list of real and imaginary risks. By the time you have heard the answer, there will be little point in asking about the benefits of the idea. The idea will have been crushed under the weight of all the risks and problems which came to light.

If you ask about the benefits first, you may find that you have to push and probe to get all the benefits of the new idea fully articulated. But establishing why the idea is a good idea changes the nature of the discussion. If the idea is rich in benefits, then it becomes worthwhile dealing with all the risks that you later identify. Your colleague will have invested personal time and effort in establishing that the idea is good, and will be less inclined to drop the idea. By identifying the benefits of the idea, your colleague will have taken ownership of the idea. People rarely oppose their own ideas.

> people rarely oppose their own ideas

2 Reinforcement: the coffee shop principle

Go down to your local coffee shop and watch people gossip. You may be able to persuade your boss that this is not just a break from work: it will help your work.

First, watch the body language. You will see that people who are deeply engrossed in conversation mirror each other's body shape. When one leans forward, the other leans forward. If one crosses his legs, the other will as well. It is like ballet without a choreographer. Everyone does it quite naturally.

Now pretend to read a newspaper while you eavesdrop on the conversations. The gossips will be busily supporting and reinforcing each others' world views. Right on cue, they will show delight, disgust, shock, surprise or sympathy with every latest revelation. They will not disbelieve what they are being told, at least not until they recount the story to someone else later. They are making it very easy to talk to each other. They are allies with common interests and common perceptions.

The same principles of reinforcement apply to business conversations. If you want someone to talk, make it easy for them to talk. Show that you are in tune with them and that you are on their side.

Start with the body language. Listening to other people's triumphs and disasters may be boring, but stay focused. Look interested. Make eye contact and stay alert: people quickly pick up lack of interest. Focus 100% of your attention on the person who is talking: when your mind wanders off to planning the next meeting, worrying about your expense claim and other matters, it shows. When you are focused, people feel flattered and will open up.

Now focus on what you say. You do not need to say much. Copy the coffee shop gossips: show that you empathise and agree with the other person. The moment you challenge them, they will close down and stop seeing you as a friend and ally. Reinforcement helps you build the rapport you need when you move on to more substantive discussions.

3 Paraphrasing

Paraphrasing is a useful way of showing understanding and building agreement. It can also be used to stop people repeating themselves.

Paraphrasing is simply a summary of what someone has said to you, expressed in your own words. This simple act achieves several goals at the same time:

- It shows that you have listened properly, and that builds empathy with the talker who wants to be heard.
- If you have misunderstood, you will quickly be corrected.
- It forces the listener to listen actively: you will look interested and the talker will respond positively to your apparent interest.

opening a notebook closes a conversation

- It helps you remember key information after the meeting: the act of saying something commits it to your short-term memory without the intrusion and formality of a notebook and pen. Opening a notebook closes a conversation: people are rarely open when they are on record.

Paraphrasing needs to be done with some care. If you say 'so what I hear you say is…' and you then repeat their words exactly you will sound like an insincere automaton. Be authentic. Use your own words to summarise what has been said. That shows you have really listened and internalised what has been said: you are more than a parrot.

For influencers, paraphrasing is most useful in one to one meetings where you want to build rapport. It can also be used in group meetings. By showing you have heard, understood and respected a colleague, you earn their respect even if you do not agree with each other. You are more likely to have a productive conversation than an argument.

Finally, paraphrasing makes windbags shut up. We have all been in meetings where there is one person who keeps on making the same point, in different ways, time and again. Everyone tries to shut him up. The more people try to stop him talking, the more he feels the need to make his point again because he feels he has not been heard. Instead of attacking such people, work with them. Let them have their say (concisely) and then summarise what was said. Even write it up on a flip chart. You have now amply shown that their point has been made and they have been heard. They can now let the meeting move on.

4 Contradiction

It was election time. We had 24 hours before the polls opened and we needed to get a last minute leaflet designed, printed and distributed overnight. And we had more or less run out of budget. No printer was going to take on a low-cost job, overnight and at great inconvenience. I called a printer and got the predictable reply: 'no'. We were stuck. Then I remembered the contradiction principle.

I went round to another printer who had worked for us before and did the normal business of establishing rapport, asking a few open questions. And then he asked, 'What can I do for you?'

'I doubt you can do anything, frankly. I have tried a couple of printers round here and they say it is impossible.'

'What's impossible?' the printer asked. He sounded slightly offended that anyone could doubt his professional expertise and his ability to do anything.

'Well,' I said with apparent reluctance, 'It's this leaflet. Still needs final design. 8,000 copies by tomorrow morning. I am told no one can do that in that amount of time.'

'Rubbish!' replied the printer who was now indignant that anyone could doubt his capability. By this time he was fully committed to proving me wrong, at any cost. Even when he heard of the pitiful budget, he was going to show me what he was capable of doing. He wanted to prove me wrong, to prove that he was better than all the other printers in town.

Mission accomplished: leaflet printed on time and to budget. Election won.

Contradiction is not about arguing with people. It is about letting people show off. Let them show how good they are. Let them prove you wrong. Contradiction is a powerful principle to use with professionals who are normally more than keen to showcase their professional talent. The trick is to make the contradiction non-confrontational: de-personalise it. Avoid saying 'I don't think this is possible' or 'I don't believe this is true'. That simply invites a win/lose argument. Since they are the experts, they will win.

The goal is contradiction, not conflict. The key to achieving this delicate balance is to de-personalise the contradiction by saying things like: 'Other printers say it is impossible to do this' or 'Finance say this profit forecast is wrong...' By doing this, you displace the blame and opprobrium onto other people: you can

> the goal is contradiction, not conflict

now work together to prove the rest of the world is wrong. You become allies, not adversaries.

5 Disclosure

A very tedious dinner engagement loomed. A colleague decided to spice it up with a wager. She bet that she could make everyone round the table, before the evening was over, reveal how they lost their virginity. Easy money. I wagered a modest amount and looked forward to collecting at the end of the evening. No one is going to reveal such intimate details to relative strangers. No chance, no way, never.

By the end of the evening, I was poorer financially and richer in knowledge. I had also disclosed a little more about myself than was perhaps wise.

Maria started by doing what she did best: asking open questions about people, reinforcing other guests by showing interest and empathy. As the evening wore on and the wine flowed, she steered the conversation to slightly more risqué areas. Occasionally, to encourage disclosure she would drop a personal indiscretion into the conversation. Competitively, the other guests would drop in even greater indiscretions. The evening was rapidly becoming more and more entertaining. Both the wine and the disclosures flowed faster and faster.

Perhaps inevitably, the discussion turned to sex. Maria told a funny story against herself. Others followed. Eventually and quite naturally, she found herself saying how she had lost her virginity. Like clockwork, everyone else followed, with suitably extravagant embellishments. Under these circumstances, I could not be the prude who said nothing. I duly followed. Social pressure made disclosure inevitable.

The moral of this tale is not that you influence strangers by telling them how you lost your virginity. The moral is that disclosure encourages disclosure.

Disclosure is a subtle art. It can be done badly. At social events it is common to spot two alpha males fighting like rutting stags. They do it through competitive disclosure. They want to outdo each other's anecdotes: who went on the most exotic holiday, who went to the most prestigious conference, who knows the most important people and who has the most air miles. Disclosure needs to be slightly more subtle and self-effacing. Tell enough to make the other person want to disclose. Let them 'win' by giving you a bigger, better and more extravagant story than yours. Never threaten or challenge their stories, even if they appear to be 98% fiction.

Summary

Listening is not a passive art. It requires skill, focus and effort to make other people talk constructively, build rapport and to become a trusted partner. No one becomes a good listener overnight; it takes effort and practice. Remember the five principles of good listening:

> no one becomes a good listener overnight; it takes effort and practice

- open and purposeful questions
- reinforcement: the coffee shop principle
- paraphrasing
- contradiction
- disclosure.

Experiment with each of the principles, one at a time. In time, they will become natural reactions.

Perhaps the easiest starting point is to avoid the three most common mistakes:

- talking over other people
- asking closed questions
- indulging in competitive anecdotes.

These are natural, but unhelpful. If you avoid these traps, you have already made a start. Talking over people and competing with anecdotes springs from the natural desire to impress. They do not impress: they irritate. Short of sticking tape across your mouth, it can be hard to not talk or compete. Even if it causes you to get blood blisters on your tongue, avoid the temptation. Instead, ask open questions and let your colleagues talk themselves into agreeing with you and admiring you.

Chapter 3

Earning the currency of influence: trust

Trust is the currency of influence. To understand how far we depend on trust, take a look at a dollar bill. It is inscribed with the words 'In God We Trust'. Regardless of faith in religion, we need faith in money. We give the dollar bill to a shopkeeper, and we both accept that it is worth a dollar. We exchange another piece of green paper and we both trust that it is worth 20 dollars. Give the shopkeeper another piece of green paper and...it will be worth nothing if it is just a green piece of paper. Trust, even more than money, makes the world go round. When trust disappears, disaster ensues. On September 14th, 2007 huge queues appeared outside the branches of one of Britain's largest mortgage lenders: Northern Rock. Trust that the bank would be able to pay its depositors vanished overnight and suddenly all its customers wanted their money back. The bank quickly went under and had to be rescued by the government: it turned out to be the overture to the Credit Crunch.

Trust is so central to our lives that we take it for granted, like breathing air. Fortunately, most of us are reasonably trusting most of the time. If we distrusted money, banks, safety of food, air travel and the water we drink, then life would become very hard. We also tend to trust each other, more or less. Twice as many people believe, as opposed to disbelieve, that the average person in the street is telling the truth. This is largely because there is no great reason for them to have to lie to us. Whether we trust them any further (like lending them $5 for a fare which they promise to mail back to us) is a moot point. In other words trust is not like an on/off switch where we either trust or do not trust someone. There are degrees of trust: trusting a stranger to tell the truth is about the weakest form of trust there is.

Trust is in the eye of the beholder. We may see ourselves as trustworthy, but that does not count. We have to be seen to be trustworthy by other people. Being in a position of authority does not automatically mean that we will be trusted. Some people in authority are trusted, others are not, as can be seen from public attitudes to different professions. The survey below asked a simple question: do you trust this profession to tell the truth?

Net 'tell the truth score' (US)	
Doctors	73%
Teachers	68%
Scientists	58%
Journalists	–19%
Trade Union Leaders	–30%
Lawyers	–41%

Adapted from Harris Poll #61 2006 'Tell the truth score' = % trust profession to tell truth
less % not trust profession to tell truth

It is as well that we trust doctors and teachers, and perhaps not surprising that we do not trust lawyers, union leaders and journalists. Politicians and stockbrokers also did very poorly, and that was before the credit crunch massacred the reputation of financial services professionals. These findings are remarkably consistent across borders. A similar (not identical) survey in the UK also put doctors and teachers as the most trusted professions. Journalists were once again near the bottom, along with politicians and business leaders.

Net 'tell the truth score' (UK)	
Doctors	80%
Teachers	69%
Average person in the street	30%
Business leaders	–26%
Journalists	–51%
Politicians	–66%

(Source: Ipsos/MORI Veracity Index 2011)

Within the workplace, trust is essential. Policy manuals and company directives can not legislate for trust. The most influential managers tend to be the most trusted: people are prepared to work with people they trust, not with people they do not trust.

> the most influential managers tend to be the most trusted

Trust has to be earned, not claimed. A short example shows how untrustworthy we sound when we claim to be trustworthy. If you heard someone saying this, how much would you trust them?

'Look, OK, John, I'm a straight sort of guy... Of course I'm an honest sort of a bloke – If I were lying...'

You can hear trust and credibility evaporating like dew in the desert as these words are said. This was Tony Blair, then Prime Minister, talking about the Iraq report on BBC Radio 4, May 13, 2005. Once you start proclaiming your honesty and trustworthiness you start to sound like a con merchant or, worse, a politician.

Trust is not some elusive pixie dust that some managers have and others lack. It is something every practising manager can acquire, with effort. Trust is the function of four variables, which we can arrange as a simple equation. Here it is, in all its spurious mathematical accuracy:

$$T = (V \times C) / (R \times D)$$

Where:

T = Trust

V = Values alignment

C = Credibility

R = Risk

D = Distance.

To understand how to build trust we need to know how to manage each of the four variables. As we start, remember that trust is built one person at a time.

1 Values alignment

The more that we appear to share common values, outlooks and priorities with someone else, the more we are likely to trust them. This can be as much social as business alignment. If two people share the same pastimes, faith, political outlook, education or experiences then they are more likely to trust each other. We may preach the values of diversity, but we prefer conformity. Diversity means challenge and is good both for society and for business. But day to day, managers prefer to work with people with whom there is the minimum chance of misunderstanding. The stunning lack of diversity at the top of most companies is the product of this conformity bias. Under 15% of board directors in the UK and USA are women, and the majority of those are in non-executive positions. Equally, if you look to the top of French, Chinese, American, or Japanese companies, they tend to be run by home country nationals. The exceptions are notable, but not typical. The overwhelming evidence is that managers prefer conformity to diversity.

This simple observation drives much behaviour. For instance, I was invited to go shooting in northern England. This was not an invitation to join an urban gang and get into a drugs war. It was an invitation to shoot some grouse on a moor. I accepted, which was a mistake on nearly every level. Guns scare me, and gun owners scare me even more. But the event was a great success, for most of the party of businessmen. They were lousy shots, which was good for the grouse. But anyone who wants to go to an event like that shares a certain world outlook: highly traditional and very right wing. So they spent the whole weekend confirming to each other that the world was in a terrible state and it needed decent people like themselves to put it right again. By the end of the weekend, they had achieved perfect values alignment with each other. They were ready to do plenty of business deals with each other because they found trust in each other.

Shooting in the office is probably not the best way to build values alignment. Fortunately, there are simpler ways of doing this.

The first step in building values alignment is to listen. The art of listening has already been covered in some detail in Chapter 2. Listening sympathetically allows the speaker to believe that you respect their world view. It also allows you to discover what that world view is. Even if there is much you dislike or disagree with, you should be able to find some areas of common ground. Focus the conversation on areas of agreement, not disagreement. Even if the only area of agreement is about your favourite films or sports, that is a start in the right direction.

> focus the conversation on areas of agreement, not disagreement

We can not pretend to have the same values as everyone else. But we can at least respect other people's values. Showing interest, and even admiration, for someone else's values, choices and lifestyle helps to build trust. Respect shows that you are not going to attack or belittle someone for who they are and what they do. And there is always something good to find in anyone. For instance, working with one politician I found he always had a good word to say for everyone he met. I watched as he was introduced to a stranger:

Politician: 'So what do you do?'

Stranger: 'I am a pawnbroker.'

I laughed inwardly. What on earth could the politician say to that? Pawnbrokers in popular mythology prey upon the weakest and most vulnerable, making money at their expense. Surely there is not much good to say there.

Politician: 'Magnificent! Pawnbrokers were the very first bankers: they started commerce as we know it. And now you provide a vital service to all those people who can not get credit anywhere else...'

As the politician spoke, I saw the pawnbroker puff himself up with pride. He had found someone who understood him and respected him. That was another vote in the bag for the politician.

If you can share the same values, or show respect for other people's values, you have made a start in building trust.

In the office, day to day, alignment is about aligning agendas and aligning priorities. Everyone believes that their own agenda is the most important and most urgent. And if you keep on shouting that you have the most important and most urgent agenda, you will find first that people shout back at you and then you hear the sound of deafening silence as people avoid you. Office life requires give and take: that does not mean you take and they give. Be clear and consistent about your needs; if something is genuinely important and urgent, say so. If you can help someone out by delaying one of your demands or finding another way of meeting your needs, do so. And make sure the other person knows that you have helped them: eventually, they will reciprocate.

2 Credibility

If you can 'talk the talk' (values alignment) you also have to 'walk the walk' (credibility). You must be able to do as you say. Credibility is as fragile as a vase: one slip and it is broken for good.

> credibility is as fragile as a vase: one slip and it is broken for good

In Shakespeare's words: 'Trust not him that hath once broken faith'(*Henry VI, Part III*, 4:4).

If we are to maintain our credibility, we have to manage expectations very carefully. It is easy to make promises without realising that we have made a promise. When the expectation is not fulfilled, we have failed even though we think we have done nothing wrong. Much of this comes down to the use of language. For instance, we may say things like:

'I will try to...'

'I hope to...'

'I will do my best...'

Clearly, we think we are not making a commitment. These are weasel words which politicians use. They give us a get out clause if things don't turn out right. But what we say and what is heard are different things. What is heard is 'I will...'. When we have tried, hoped and done our best but not been able to deliver, we have just failed to live up to a perceived commitment. We have to make sure we set the right perceptions and expectations. If we are not sure that we can do something we need to be clearer: weasel words are not enough. We have to spell out precisely why something may not be possible and when we will find out whether we really can do it or not.

Even when we say nothing, we can lose credibility. Annual reviews are a critical moment when bosses build or lose trust with their team. Team members can take bad news, but they find it hard to accept surprises. If you have kept quiet, or been evasive about a team member's weaknesses you will find the annual review will be problematic. If you suddenly discover honesty in the annual review, the reviewee will be in shock and denial. If you have been honest throughout the year, and given clear feedback and support then you will have managed expectations well: bad news will not be a surprise. Being honest throughout the year builds credibility and respect. Team members hate ambiguity and uncertainty. Being clear about performance allows them to improve in good time.

The path to credibility parts company with the path to popularity. The path to popularity ends in weakness. In the short term you become popular by saying nice things and supporting people; but if you can not deliver on your implied promises of support, then you lose credibility and trust. In the short term you can become popular by doing people favours, having sweets at your desk for passers-by, letting people slip their deadlines and targets. But in the end you are only as popular as your latest favour: you become ever weaker.

The path to credibility means that you need to have the difficult conversation early. Normally, a difficult conversation is no more than a professional conversation. Two examples will make the point:

- A team member wants promotion. The populist manager will hint that they will do their best to secure promotion, as long as the team member is loyal and hard working. The credible manager will have the difficult conversation early and will set out exactly what the team member needs to do, how long it is likely to take, and what the odds of success really are.

- You are proposing a new idea or project. The boss or client wants the project at the lowest possible price. The populist manager will find ways of cutting corners to cut the price. As a result, the project may fail. The credible manager will work through the budget and show exactly what the consequences of cutting the budget will be.

Building influence is about building credibility, not popularity. And in the cases above, each difficult conversation builds respect. The team member or boss will recognise that they are having a professional and constructive discussion. At the end of it, you will both have expectations which you share and are realistic.

> building influence is about building credibility, not popularity

The process of building credibility is slow. If we believe the average person in the street, it is because we have not had the chance to be let down by them. Going from that weak-form trust to strong-form trust takes time. In practice, we have countless opportunities to prove our credibility and trustworthiness. After a first meeting we can send a quick summary, or a thank you note, or follow up on an action point on the same day. By doing so, we put down a marker that we can be trusted. If someone leaves a message for us, we build credibility by replying fast. If we have to be reminded to reply, or if we have to be reminded about an action point, we lose credibility. From these very small beginnings, we can move on to larger demonstrations of credibility.

The higher the stakes, the more important it is to manage expectations and to deliver on our promises. For team members, promises of promotions, assignments and bonuses are very high stakes. And humans being humans, we tend to hear what we want to hear. We want to hear that we are going to get the best assignment, the next promotion and the best bonus: we will certainly believe that we deserve it. Against these expectations, managers have to be brutally honest and clear. It feels awkward to be so clear and honest, but is a far better way of building respect and credibility than by disappearing into the jungle of vague words and half promises.

Credibility and values intimacy drive trust up over time. There are also two things which drive trust down: risk and distance. We have to manage these as actively as we manage our credibility and demonstrate our values.

3 Risk

Risk is the rust in trust. It is corrosive of our ability to trust people. The higher the risk, the less inclined we are to trust strangers. In the veracity surveys above we saw that most of us will trust strangers to tell the truth. Unless we wish to achieve great poverty, we are unlikely to trust a stranger with our life savings.

Within the workplace there are two ways we can use risk to advantage. We can reduce it or raise it.

A good way to manage risk is to raise it, selectively. If a new course of action looks risky, people will naturally prefer to do nothing. The response may be to reduce the perceived risk of the new idea. Equally valid is to raise the perceived risk of doing nothing. When doing nothing looks extremely risky, people start looking for alternatives. If necessary, create the crisis and focus people on its dire consequences. This is what the President of a global electronics firm did to great effect. The firm was in crisis, under the onslaught of Asian competition. To survive, the firm needed a major cost cutting drive. The President issued a simple

> a good way to manage risk is to raise it

message: 20% off costs, 20% off working capital, 20% off headcount by year end.

The first reaction was that all the division heads identified all the logical risks and reasons why the goals were unachievable. For instance:

- We have just cut by 20% so surely we can not cut again.
- We are growing by 20% so that means we should not have to make any cuts.
- We already have the best benchmark costs in the industry, so we should not cut.
- We are R&D/marketing/sales and the future of the company, so you can not cut us.

These were all rational and logical objections. If the President had accepted them, the firm would now be bankrupt: when you accept excuses, you accept failure. The risks and problems that the division heads identified were rational and logical, but would have led the firm to bankruptcy.

The President decided to raise the stakes and raise the risk of doing nothing. To his list of 20% cuts he added one more cut for the division heads to think about: 'If you do not deliver the 20% cut, you will be part of the 20%.' Suddenly, the risk of doing nothing soared compared to the risk of taking on the 20%. More widely, he made it clear that the choice was not between 20% cuts or no cuts. It was between 20% cuts and 100% cuts which come from bankruptcy.

Cutting 20% of staff sounds terrible. But going bankrupt (the banks wanted their money back) and getting wiped out by foreign competition was even worse. If the choice was losing 20% of jobs or no job losses, everyone would have stayed with the status quo. When the choice was to lose 20% of jobs or 100% of jobs, the 20% option started to look a lot more attractive.

Most organisations and managers resist change because change is riskier than doing nothing. Increasing the perceived risk of doing nothing alters that equation in favour of change.

The more conventional way of managing the perception of risk is to reduce it. The key is to understand that risk is not just logical: it is emotional and personal. Project managers who fall in love with their risk and issue logs miss the point. Their logical risks can be managed away with appropriate remedial actions. The killer risks are personal:

- How will this idea affect me and my prospects?
- How much effort will I have to put in?
- How will I look if this idea succeeds or fails?

When colleagues object to an idea they will use rational objections, because managers have to pretend to be rational. This is what the President's division heads did: they used rational objections to try to stop something which they personally did not like. This opens up a huge bear trap for managers. Fighting emotional objections with logical answers is like fighting fire with fuel: it normally ends in tears.

> fighting emotional objections with logical answers is like fighting fire with fuel

The influential manager will learn to separate out rational from emotional responses. Truly logical risks have a pattern all of their own:

- They will not be a surprise: the more creative and unexpected the challenge, the more likely it is to be a rational objection hiding an emotional fear.
- They will be presented positively: 'how do we deal with ...' rather than 'it's impossible because...'
- They lead to a discussion of solutions.
- They come in small doses, rather than vast hordes of objections.

Logical risks can be dealt with logically. Emotional risks need to be dealt with emotionally. The electronics President had an effective way of doing this: raise the stakes personally for each division head. In less traumatic times it pays to reduce the perceived risks. This is a combination of active listening and the art of the persuasive conversation, which are covered in Chapters 1 and 2. These are discussions which are only productive in private. In public, managers have to maintain the rational façade. In private, they can be more open about their personal interests and agenda.

4 Distance

Distance is the opposite of values intimacy and credibility. The greater the distance between two people, the less likely they are to trust each other. There are four main types of distance:

- distance between what we say and what we mean
- distance between what we say and what is heard
- distance between your interests and my interests
- distance between my background, experience and values and yours.

What we say and what we mean

Politicians and advertisers share a talent for saying things which are technically true, but completely misleading. Anyone who has been attracted by offers of 'flights to Rome from $40' will have entered a world where the offer is only available a year in advance, going to an airport 100km from Rome in the middle of the night, and the offer excludes endless extras such as booking fees, fuel surcharge, taxes, credit card fee and surcharges for luggage and assigned seating. And if a politician is caught lying, they resort to saying they 'mis-spoke' or committed a 'terminological inexactitude'. Then they wonder why we don't trust them. They may mislead us once, but we will be twice as careful if we have to listen to them again.

George Orwell predicted the rise of doublespeak in his novel *1984*, where ministries did the opposite of what they were labelled. For instance:

- Ministry of Peace: responsible for continuous war
- Ministry of Plenty: responsible for rationing
- Ministry of Truth: responsible for propaganda
- Ministry of Love: responsible for suppression and torture of dissidents.

The business world is quickly following the political world, using words to avoid saying it straight. The 12 most dangerous, and misleading words in business are:

1 Just
   This is used to make a huge request or error seem trivial as in: 'Could you just do this (500 page) document by Monday?' It is a request best made late on a Friday afternoon.

2 But
   Remember, whatever is said before 'but' is baloney, as in 'That was a great presentation, but...', or 'I would like to help, but...'

3 From
   Much loved by advertisers, as in 'broadband from $10 per month...' for three months before the price jumps, and it excludes connection, excludes compulsory landline rental and more. Also, 'flights from...' 'smartphones from...' 'bespoke kitchens from...'. When you hear 'from' be worried for your wallet.

4 Might (and any other conditional verb)
   Might is used to achieve two things: first it sets up a negotiating position as in, 'I might be able to do that if...' Second, it lays the groundwork for excusing failure later on: 'I would have done it, if only...'

5 **Only**
   Closely related to 'just', it is an attempt to make a big request
   or problem seem small. 'It was *only* a small error...we *only*
   dropped one nuclear bomb over London...'

6 **Important (and urgent)**
   Used to puff up any presentation: 'This important new
   product/initiative...' Important to whom? And why? Maybe it
   is important to the speaker, but why is it to me?

7 **Strategic**
   Important, with bells on. See Strategic Human Capital
   division, formerly known as the Personnel Department.
   Alternatively used to justify something which has no financial
   justification at all: 'This strategic IT investment... (which costs
   $100 million and has no identifiable payback at all) is essential
   to the survival of the business.'

8 **Rightsize, downsize, best shore, offshore, outsource, optimise,
   redeploy, downshift, re-engineer**
   How many ways are there of avoiding saying straight up: we
   are going to lay off staff?

9 **Thank you**
   Normally 'thank you' is good, except when used by automated
   voices at call centres saying, 'Thank you for calling, we value
   your call... (and we have so much contempt for our customers
   that we can not be bothered to answer your call promptly, so
   we will put you on hold until you give up and try to use our
   impenetrable and useless online help instead).'

10 **Interesting**
   Fear this word. When your lawyer uses it, you are doomed.
   When your doctor uses it, check your will is up to date. The
   recession is certainly interesting. A slightly less interesting time
   would be preferable.

11 **Opportunity**
   Because the word 'problem' has been banned in business
   speak, all problems have become opportunities. This means

many opportunities are problems. There is a limit to how many opportunities I can solve. Interesting and strategic opportunities really scare me.

12 Investment

'Investment' was first hijacked by the British government to justify wild and uncontrolled public sector spending. Spending is bad, but investment is good, so they simply re-classify spending as investment and make the bad sound good.

There is some good news in this. The more that jargon and weasel words become endemic, the less managers are trusted. This creates space for managers who use plain words and say what they mean to stand out from the rest of the pack. Sometimes, the art of influence is not too sophisticated. Do the basics right and you can be noticeably different and better than colleagues who try to be clever.

The distance between what we say and what is heard

Most of us do not set out to be dishonest. But we can inadvertently set expectations which we can not meet, as shown in the section on credibility. The problem is not what we say: it is what our colleagues decide to hear. If in doubt, overcommunicate. Steve, who ran a life insurance firm, developed the rule of five to cope with this problem: 'Do not think anyone has understood anything until they have heard it at least five times'. His rationale for the rule of five was:

- First time: statement not heard amid the noise of other messages
- Second time: statement heard but ignored
- Third time: statement heard but not really believed
- Fourth time: statement heard, believed and not acted on
- Fifth time: they might actually do something.

Besides repetition, consistency and accuracy are essential. Assume that people hear what they want to hear: they will misinterpret what you say to minimise the downside and maximise the upside.

If you say something differently five times, they will hear whichever version they want to hear. If you are consistent, there is only one message they can hear.

The distance between my interests and your interests

The distance between your interests is the opposite of values intimacy. 80% of survey respondents (BBC Ipsos/MORI 2009) believe that politicians act mainly in their own interest or the interests of their party: few people believe they act in the interests of the country or their constituents. Equally, the scandals over excessive CEO pay make many fear that CEOs are acting mainly in their own interest, not in the interests of staff or shareholders. Business leaders and politicians rank low on perceived veracity.

To close the gap we need to act with selfless independence, at least occasionally. We need to show that we understand, respect and if necessary adapt to the needs of other people. If all we ever do is to chase our own interests, then few people will feel the need to trust us.

influencers learn to collaborate rather than compete across the firm

Organisations are designed around competing and conflicting interests. Each function and department has a different set of priorities and perspectives. As we shall see later, influencers learn to collaborate rather than compete across the firm.

The distance between my background and yours

A consistent theme throughout *How to Influence and Persuade* is the desire for intimacy and conformity. We find it far easier to deal with people like ourselves, because we think we understand such people. Diversity sounds good in politicians' speeches, but even they do not practise it. The vast majority choose to live in single race marriages: daytime diversity leads to sunset segregation.

Even in firms with a strong conformist culture, different people are...different. Age alone is a great divider in everything from personal priorities, experience and taste in music. Asking a 60-year-old and a 20-year-old to listen to each others' music is normally a recipe for pain and disbelief.

The easiest way to reduce the background gap is to listen actively. Even if you do not share their world view, by listening you show you respect them. You also learn about them and can find a few areas in common: build on what is common, not on what is different.

Summary

Trust is the invisible force behind the invisible hand of influence. It has to be invisible. The more you talk about trust openly, the less trustworthy you seem: you will sound like a politician. Some people carry the aura of trust around them, others do not. But there is no mystery to this aura. Building and using trust comes down to the simple trust equation:

$$T = (V \times C) / (R \times D)$$

The mathematics may not be sound but the logic is: values intimacy and credibility build trust; risk and distance weaken trust. It is an equation which can be used to build the most productive relationships of all: the high trust partnerships.

Chapter 4
Act the part

Try this simple test. Who would you be more likely to trust:

A: Ripped jeans, matted hair, stubble, dirty fingernails, mumbles and is late into work.

B: Well pressed suit, clean, shaven, attentive, focused, energetic and positive.

If you chose Type B you may have put your trust in bankers who have blown billions while lining their pockets; you may have trusted politicians who buy floating duck houses for their garden and have their moat cleaned at public expense. And that perhaps makes the point. Type A might be your IT genius who has just been up all night preventing system melt down, but we are still inclined to trust Type B. Appearances matter. Call it 'career gear' or 'dress for success': first impressions count.

Put simply, if we want to be influential, we have to act and look influential. We need to be perceived the right way. Perceptions may be wrong, but the consequences of those perceptions are real. Perception management is essential.

Perception management is a combination of how you behave and how you look. There is argument about how quickly people judge each other when they first meet. Some claim it takes three minutes to form a judgement. Others say it takes just three seconds. Either way, it is clear that first impressions count. With that in mind, we will explore five themes:

1 Act the part.

2 Look the part.

3 Speak the part: pace, space and grace.

4 Empathy, engagement and eye contact.

5 Make the right first impressions: networking.

The art of influence is not just about what you do. It is about how you are, how you are seen and judged. You need more than just the box of influencing tools and tricks to succeed. You need to be seen as someone people value, trust and want to work with. If you are seen that way, then you have opened the doors to influence. If you are seen the wrong way, then no matter how many tools and tricks you may have mastered, you will find the doors to influence stay firmly shut.

Being seen the right way does not guarantee success. Being seen the wrong way guarantees failure. Acting the part is a precondition of successful influencing.

Act the part

Every organisation has its own unwritten rules of survival and success. You need to decode those unwritten rules for yourself. Some of the common questions include:

- How late should I really work?
- Should I take initiative and risk, or keep my nose clean and follow the process?
- What do I really need permission for, and what do I just get on with?
- How should I dress?
- What sort of jokes can we tell, to whom and when: or are we Very Serious?
- How deferential should I be to the big bosses?

You can search in vain through policy manuals for answers to these questions. Everyone knows the rules, but no one will tell you. They will not even tell you what the questions are: you have to get the answers to the exam right without knowing the questions.

A firm's rules of survival and success are mandatory etiquette. Ignore them at your peril. To act the part you have to find out your organisation's real rules of survival and success. Do not read the values statement. If in doubt, watch the feet not the mouth: deeds speak truer than words. Look at who is promoted and why; who gets the biggest bonuses and best assignments and why; look at who gets fired or 'let go'. These actions will tell you what is really expected of you. Quite often the rules of survival and success involve knowing when and how to break which rules. To make things happen it is often easier to ask forgiveness than to ask for permission: act first, ask for permission later.

Beyond the fog of confusing signals around how you are meant to behave, there are a few universal traits of influential people who stand out from their peers. They all share the three Es of good presenters, leaders and influencers. They have:

- Energy
- Enthusiasm
- Excitement.

If you are not enthusiastic, no one will be enthusiastic for you or your idea. In the drab world of Planet Office, enthusiasm is seen as a certifiable disease. No one is enthusiastic, which is why you can stand out by showing some enthusiasm, energy and excitement for what you do. Corporate defences have become very sophisticated in dealing with presentations, spreadsheets, meetings and the normal tools of organisation life. But the corporate defences are very weak

> if you are not enthusiastic, no one will be enthusiastic for you

when it comes to enthusiasm. The chances are that somewhere in your organisation's value statement there is a call to be passionate about whatever your organisation does. The call to passion is completely ignored, except for the odd late-night liaison: and that is not what the values statement is advocating. If you can live the values around passion, you will be ahead of your colleagues. And there is a severe risk that you may also start to enjoy what you do. You will live better and work better as a result.

Put this the other way around. How often have you been favourably influenced by someone who lacks interest in what they do, mumbles in a boring voice and looks distracted?

In the film *Flash Gordon*, the evil Emperor Ming sent out a command on the eve of his wedding: 'All creatures shall make merry! On pain of death!' Telling people to be merry, or be enthusiastic, energetic and excited is perhaps unhelpful when faced with yet another urgent but humdrum deadline like the month end close.

So here are some things you can do to help you.

Look the part

If you act with energy, enthusiasm and excitement you are likely to be forgiven most sartorial disasters. There is an old adage which says that you are never poorly dressed if you wear a smile. But we should not make it hard for ourselves. If we dress the part, it makes it far easier for people to believe us.

In some cases, it is very easy to follow the dress code and look authoritative. The armed forces give their senior officers plenty of gold braid and medals. Their crisp uniforms exude crisp authority. I discovered the full power of dress when I ventured into the Highlands of Papua New Guinea. I first met the tribe in a ramshackle town. The tribesmen were wearing their best clothes for town: second hand clothes inherited from western charity donors. They looked evil. I had no idea who their leader was: they all looked as menacing as each other.

Two days later I reached their village in the distant highlands. They changed out of their town clothes. Suddenly, it was easy to see who the chief was. He was the one wearing a head dress made of huge bird of paradise feathers, and he was bedecked in cowrie shells and other exotic imports from the coast. He looked magnificent, even regal. In town he had looked like a tramp or potential mugger. Same person in different dress gave a different message.

In the business world it is perhaps best not to wear gold braid, medals and bird of paradise feathers in your hair. We need some other way of appearing authoritative and influential. The problem is that dress codes are becoming ever more ambiguous. There has been a sartorial revolution since the days when grey socks would have been seen as subversive. At a recent conference of a global high tech firm, everyone from the CEO downwards wore jeans and T-shirts. In government offices, senior officials still cling to the orthodoxy of a suit and tie. Both situations demand conformity: to act the part, it helps to conform to whatever the dress code may be.

The principles of dress codes are the same as the principles of all etiquette. Etiquette is not about arcane rules over where to put the fish knives. Etiquette should be about providing rules which put everyone on an equal footing, and put everyone at ease. The same goes for dress codes. The goal is to put your colleagues at ease: they should feel comfortable being seen with you and talking to you. Given the variety and ambiguity of dress codes, there is no simple answer to how you should appear. However, there are some guiding principles:

- mirroring: conformity
- conservatism
- aspiration.

Mirroring and conformity is the key principle: dress how others dress. If everyone else is dressing in T-shirt and jeans, you should probably follow. Dressing in a suit and tie would mark you out as a stuffy weirdo. Equally, if you go to a formal black tie event, wearing a T-shirt and jeans is simply insulting to everyone else who has made the effort to dress up. T-shirts and formal suits are simply different styles of conformity.

> t-shirts and formal suits are simply different styles of conformity

Conservatism: if in doubt, err on the side of caution and formality. This applies particularly to people who are down the pecking order of power: suppliers, vendors and junior staff. For instance, consultants tend to dress slightly more conservatively than their clients. They need to look trustworthy and reliable. All the greatest rogues, from bankers to tyrants and politicians dress in sober suits and ties. It is their camouflage to make them appear trustworthy. It works all too often.

Aspiration: this is particularly useful for more junior staff. Look at how people one or two levels above you dress. The chances are they spend more money, time and effort on their personal appearance. If you want to join the club, it pays to follow the club dress rules. If in doubt, mirror the example of senior people, not junior people. Judging people on how they dress is both absurd and unfair, but who said the world is fair?

Speak the part: pace, space and grace

Try to remember some conferences or training events you went to over the last year or two. Now try to remember something about the trainers and presenters. The chances are that you remember very little about their carefully crafted PowerPoint slides. But you will remember them for how they looked, how they acted and how they spoke. And that is how you will be remembered as well. You will be remembered for how you were as much as for what you did.

> you will be remembered for how you were as much as for what you did

We all think we know how to speak well because we are speaking for much of the day. But if we are asked to speak to an audience of 500, suddenly we discover that the simple art of speaking is not quite so simple at all. Speaking to influence is different from speaking socially. Formal presentations are an art in their own right: they are set piece events where the speaker forms lasting impressions on those in the audience. For this reason, presentations merit a separate chapter. But even in day-to-day meetings it pays to speak well.

At extremes, public figures such as Margaret Thatcher have taken elocution lessons to change their accent, tone and pitch. You do not need to go that far. A few simple rules will move you ahead of most of your colleagues when it comes to speaking at meetings and speaking in public.

When speaking at meetings, remember the original motto of Jaguar cars when it was founded by Sir William Lyons: 'pace, space and grace'. That is how you should speak: with pace, space and grace.

Pace is not about speaking fast. It is about speaking slow. Speak with purpose. Research on the great speakers such as Churchill, Kennedy and Mandela shows that they speak much more slowly than most people: nearer 110 words a minute against 120–150 words a minute in normal speech. Martin Luther King spoke just 88 words in the first minute of his 'I have a dream' speech. As an exercise, try repeating his speech at his speed (88 words a minute). And then try saying it at gabbling speed of 250 words a minute. You will still make sense at speed, but the meaning and weight will be lost:

> *I have a dream*
>
> *That one day this nation will rise up and live out the true meaning of its creed:*
>
> *'We hold these truths to be self-evident that all men are created equal'*
>
> *I have a dream*

That one day on the red hills of Georgia

Sons of former slaves

And sons of former slave owners

Will be able to sit down together at the table of brotherhood

I have a dream

That one day, even the state of Mississippi

A state sweltering with the heat of injustice...

Going slowly adds weight to each word and, by extension, to the speaker. Note also that his speech is full of short words and there is no management jargon. Jargon impresses no one except the speaker.

> jargon impresses no one except the speaker

Use plain English: it is more powerful and direct than the contortions of management-speak jargon. By contrast, someone who is speaking at 250 words a minute sounds manic. Clearly, if you only ever speak slowly, you will sound odd. It pays to mix it up: varying pace and pitch will keep people engaged. But if you have something important to say, slow right down so that the message comes across with clarity and emphasis.

Space and grace also counts when speaking. Space means having the courage not to fill the air with noise. If you are asked a question, be ready to pause and consider your answer. You will not look hesitant: you will look thoughtful and your response will have more weight and authority. Not speaking is hard to achieve. When there is a pause in a meeting, there is always someone who is desperate to pollute the air with whatever thoughts may be escaping their brain via their mouth. Influencing is about listening as much as it is about talking.

Grace is in short supply. We all feel pressured. We all need to make our point. Meetings can become competitive: power barons defending their space, people trying to score points off each other and look smarter than the next person. You can enter that competition if you want. But the best way to win is by not competing, or by not being seen to compete. Rise above the competition. Be graceful. Don't try to compete with other people's insights: thank them for their insights. You immediately win a friend and make it impossible for them to argue with you.

Pace, space and grace in influential meetings

Francis is one of the smartest people I know. He is smart enough to hide his smartness. Less confident and less smart people would want to prove their smartness at every opportunity by scoring points. Francis deploys his smartness with grace. In a meeting where five people have somehow managed to come up with seven conflicting view points, Francis will stay silent and listen: the hallmark of a good influencer. He gives people space to argue against each other. Slowly, everyone argues themselves into a brooding, grudging stalemate. Then Francis is ready to strike.

Carefully, he summarises the discussion as he has heard it. He uses paraphrasing, like all good influencers. He has the grace to thank each person for the wonderful insight that they offered. As he does so, you see each person puff themselves up with pride: their innate genius has just been recognised in public. Of course, his summary is partial. He picks out the comments that he finds most useful to his own point of view. By the time he has finished, each person feels that they have been heard and that their unique talent has been recognised. They are ready to agree to more or less anything Francis suggests, and they do.

Francis wins without competing. He wins twice: he wins the argument and he wins friends. More traditional persuaders might win the argument, but they will not win many friends. And they will find it much harder to win next time, while Francis will find it much easier. Pace, space and grace works in meetings, especially when used with the other influencing skills of listening and paraphrasing.

Empathy, engagement and eye contact

We have all been in meetings where colleagues are looking over our shoulder, texting while pretending to pay attention and generally showing that they are not at all interested in proceedings. It rarely makes a good impression.

In contrast, we can all remember the times when we have been centre stage, under the spotlight in a meeting. Everyone is paying attention, and suddenly every word, every action seems more vivid and more memorable.

You do not influence people positively by ignoring them and focusing on your text messages. You influence people by engaging them. That means you have to pay attention to them: we all know when colleagues are paying attention or not, so make the effort.

The easiest way to show you are paying attention is with your eyes. Make eye contact. Billy Graham, the great American preacher, used it to devastating effect. How do you engage hundreds of people with eye contact? One person at a time, that's how. He did not look blankly at the sea of faces in front of him. Each phrase, each sentence would be addressed directly to one person in the audience. It was electrifying to find that you were being addressed directly and in person by the great man. Once engaged, you stayed engaged.

Use eye contact even when not speaking. Instead of shuffling papers at a meeting, keep your focus on the speaker. You will hear more, understand more and look more engaged than the other people who are scribbling notes, checking mobile phones beneath the table or gazing out of the window. As you look at someone, you will probably find that you unconsciously mirror their body movements. When they lean forward, you will too. This appears empathetic and engaged. Other people who are not engaged may well be leaning back, fiddling about. The more you look at them, the more likely you are to mirror their behaviour and look disengaged. And once you look disengaged, you probably become disengaged as well. The mind switches off when the body does, and vice versa. Choosing where to look has impact.

If you want a change of view, look at the chairperson. You will probably pick up how they are reacting. And the chairperson will notice you, making it much easier for you to intervene when you want.

Make the right first impressions

If you know how to look and act the part, you are well on the way to making a good first impression. But special situations require special preparation. Two occasions when you will need to make a strong first impression are:

- meeting someone for the first time (selling or interviewing, for instance)
- networking.

Remember that you make an impression even before you meet someone. If your initial email is sloppy and pitched the wrong way, you have just made a bad impression before you have even met. If you are starting your own company and have nothing, be prepared to invest in good quality letterhead, a good brochure and a good website. Make it look professional. People are wary of dealing with start ups, so look bigger, more established and more substantial than you are. Project confidence and professionalism to the rest of the world.

> you make an impression even before you meet someone

Meeting someone for the first time

I found myself responsible for recruiting business school graduates to a high-end strategy firm. Some candidates were easy: they were great or they were disasters. Most were in the middle: they seemed to tick all the boxes, but we could not make our minds up about them. I found a very easy way of making the decision: I asked my personal assistant, who would have walked them to and from reception. It only took a couple of minutes, but most candidates revealed themselves in that time, with their defences down. Assuming that personal assistants do not matter is a fatal error. Subsequent events indicated that she had about a 90% success rate in picking winners, which was better than the rest of the selection team put together.

Here is what she looked for:

- The three Es: energy, excitement and enthusiasm. Even if they were nervous, that was OK, as long as they had the three Es

- The fourth E: expertise. Did they actually know anything about our firm? Some candidates showed total ignorance. Others used the walk to slip in a couple of insightful questions, hoping to get a reality check from the personal assistant. Smart move, much appreciated.

- The fifth E: engagement. Some candidates took the time to exchange pleasantries with my assistant and treat her like a human being. Others behaved as if she was invisible and did not matter. She was visible and she did matter, as they later found out to their cost.

If you have the five Es it is quite hard to go far wrong. If in doubt, let people talk about their favourite subject: themselves.

Networking

Some people love networking events. True extroverts draw energy and inspiration from the opportunity to meet new people. Many of the rest of us cringe at the thought of drinking cheap wine in a sea of people we have never met before. Even at corporate conferences, most people do not network easily. Most people stick to seeing people they already know: IT people talk to IT people and sales people talk to sales people. There is also a geographic split: Paris staff talk to Paris staff, Tokyo staff talk to Tokyo staff. And generally speaking, senior people talk among themselves and junior people talk among themselves. The corporate event may be a gathering of the tribes, but all the tribes still stick to their own kind.

These events are ideal for building influence. They are a chance to meet people you would otherwise struggle to get an introduction to. But networking success is not a matter of luck. Going to an event and hoping to meet interesting and useful people might work socially, but is unlikely to help you meet the people you need to meet. You have to work for it.

So how can anyone network successfully?

A good start is to do your homework. In a sea of 300 faces, there are probably going to be three or four people you would like to meet. Find out who will be there and who you need to meet. Turn the networking event from a random social event into a targeted business event.

The next step is to make your introduction to the person you want to meet. I have found the best way of meeting someone is by an introduction: find someone who can introduce you directly. If this is not possible, then at least make sure you have identified the person correctly. Even if you have Googled your target and seen their picture, linking the picture to the sea of faces is not so easy. And mistakes happen. As a back up, I normally ask if anyone has seen Mr X or Mrs Y who I want to meet. There will always be someone who can point you to X and Y, which at least avoids the embarrassment of introducing yourself very confidently to the wrong person.

The next step is often the hardest: saying hello to a stranger. The more important the stranger is, the harder this becomes in our own minds. So here are four easy ways of introducing yourself to an important stranger:

- Congratulate them. If you have done your homework, you should be able to find something interesting they have done or said recently. Few people can resist such personalised flattery and you will quickly find that they are keen to hear more from you.

- Ask them to talk about their favourite subject: themselves. If you have done your homework, this is easy: 'I heard that you have been doing some very interesting work on X, which interests me because...tell me more...'

- Ask directly about your interest: 'I am working on X, and would like to get your advice on X, or meet you about it...'

- Use your personal introduction: 'So-and-so suggested that we should get together because...'

Alert readers will notice that the first two steps of networking are the same as the first two steps of the persuasive conversation: do your homework and then build rapport or alignment. In practice, the networking discussion tends to short circuit the persuasive conversation. Cocktails and canapés are not normally the place to make your big pitch for your great new idea: all you want is to set up a time when you can meet formally to discuss your idea further. To do this focus on how you would like to help them (how your idea will help them) and then suggest setting up a meeting later. Social convention makes it hard for anyone to refuse. Job done.

Summary

If you always mess up and let people down, you will be remembered for all the wrong reasons. Otherwise, you will be remembered more for how you are than what you have achieved. If you beat budget by 7%, hit a deadline and make a clever point you will remember these things. Your colleagues will remember much more about how you are: are you collaborative, supportive, enthusiastic and engaging? Or are you untrustworthy, duplicitous, negative and competitive?

Acting the part should not be unnatural. It should be about finding the best of who you are. We can all be enthusiastic and energetic at times. We can all be supportive and collaborative when we want to be. The challenge is to do these consistently, and especially when the going gets tough. To sustain the right behaviours we have to find the right context in which we can flourish. If we are working in a place which brings out our dark side, it is time to find another place to work.

All organisations are tribal, and all tribes have their own rituals which they jealously guard. No one set of dress or behaviour is better than another. All that matters is whether you choose to conform to the tribal rituals or rebel against them. Your first challenge is to work out what the rules of survival and success are in your organisation. The rules that count are not written down anywhere: only trivial rules such as expenses policy are put down in writing.

> acting the part does not guarantee success: it is a precondition of success

As an influential person, you need to be someone that people want to work with, not someone people have to work with. Acting the part does not guarantee success: it is a precondition of success. Once you become someone that colleagues want to work with, you have created the conditions in which all the other tools of the influencing can work.

Chapter 5

Win–win–win

Managers compete heavily for the same limited pot of management time, budget, bonus and promotion. The real competition is not in the market place: it is sitting at a desk near you. The result is a macho world of win–lose. As ever, however, the best way to win is without fighting. This is the subtle art of the win–win–win. The win–win–win is a win for you, a win for your colleague and a win for the organisation. If you use influence well, most battles can be avoided. The art is to win while letting the other side think that they have won as well. The art of the win–win–win is a basic principle of negotiation, both within the firm and with third parties.

> the real competition is not in the market place: it is sitting at a desk near you

The five main strands of achieving a win–win–win discussion are:

1 Focus on interests, not positions.

2 Offer options.

3 Craft a story.

4 Argue in private, agree in public.

5 Give and take.

Win-win-win and the soup tin labels

These five themes can be found in the unlikely world of selling labels for soup tins.

Selling labels for soup tins is not glamorous, but it is necessary. Inevitably, the buyer wanted a lower price. He always wanted a lower price. That is all he could think about because that is how he showed he was doing a good job. The salesman had to maximise his selling price. Every meeting became an argument. Both sides had a very clear position which could be expressed as a price.

One day, the salesman did something odd. He asked if he could tour the soup plant: he wanted to see what happened to his labels. Relieved to have a discussion that was not an argument, the buyer agreed. They toured the factory and talked to various managers about what they wanted from the soup labels. The scheduler was frustrated: it was very difficult to predict demand. He often needed quick turnaround on the supply of labels: if there was a cold snap, then soup sales would soar and they would run out of soup labels. Labels represented 0.1% of the cost of the soup, but without the label, they would lose 100% of the sales.

The marketing manager was also frustrated. He often needed short runs for promotions or for test markets. Like the scheduler, the cost of the labels was more or less irrelevant. He needed flexible design and fast turnaround. The production manager, meanwhile, cursed the marketing manager. To be efficient, he wanted nice long runs of tomato soup. All the changing over between flavours and designs was a pain in the backside which interrupted the efficient flow of production.

The vendor and the buyer returned to the office thoughtfully. Perhaps the label maker could do more to help the soup maker: short runs, quick turnaround and flexible design seemed to be at least as important as price. Suddenly the vendor and buyer had more to talk about. The label maker could help the soup maker sell more and make more money by offering short runs and quick turnarounds. And the soup maker would pay more for this. This allowed the salesman to offer a further reduction on the price of labels for long runs of tomato soup: he was making up for that price concession with price gains elsewhere. In return he got guarantees of long runs and high volumes. The label maker won (higher prices on special runs) and the buyer won (helped the soup company make more money).

The soup story illustrates the main points of a successful win-win:

- *Interests not positions*: the price argument was win-lose. Helping the soup manufacturer make money was a win–win.
- *Offer options*: move the discussion away from price and onto other things which might be of value to the soup maker.
- *Argue in private, agree in public*: The negotiations took place in the buyer's office. If they had taken place elsewhere in the factory, the buyer would have found it difficult to be so flexible.
- *Craft a story*: the salesman was giving the buyer a chance to show he was not just tough (on price) but he was also smart (improving firm profitability). The win was not just a rational win for the company: it was a personal win for the buyer.
- *Give and take*: By creating options, the salesman was able to offer concessions on price (for tomato soup labels) and gain a return on both volumes (tomato soup) and on price (special runs).

The vendor had been used to the old ways of persuading: the win–lose discussion on price. By using the skills of influence, he became more effective at influencing. The relationship between the salesman and buyer became less confrontational and more collaborative.

Below, we will explore how to apply these five principles of influencing in practice.

Focus on interests, not positions

The most vicious arguments are win–lose arguments. What is at stake is not just the rational outcome about who gets the better part of the deal. There is also a huge amount of emotional capital at stake: who is seen to have won? The best way to win any war is without fighting. Instead of using force, use creativity to change the rules of engagement.

> the best way to win any war is without fighting

Telling people to get creative is not helpful. And creativity workshops do not help either: they give creativity a bad name. Being asked what sort of flower you would be if you were a flower is bad enough. Acting the flower is worse. Fortunately, there is method to being creative when it comes to influential discussions. The principle is simple: find the interests behind the position. Below are some classic positions which set up a win-lose argument:

Position	Counter-position
I want a 25% pay rise	Policy only allows a 5% rise
Give me a 20% discount on this purchase	No, I can't make a loss
Cut your budget 10% for next year	There is nothing left to cut
I want to be promoted	No promotions are available

The challenge is to understand the interest which lies behind the position. To start with, look at the example below of the classic pay and promotion discussion.

Turning a pay and promotion discussion into a win–win–win

Sarah taught in a challenging inner city school. She had done extremely well in her first two years at the school. She felt she was now due a pay rise and a promotion. The head teacher had little budget and not much flexibility on grades and promotions. Sarah and the head teacher had completely opposite positions: pay rise and promotion versus no rise and no promotion. War loomed. How could they avoid a win-lose battle over their respective positions?

Fortunately, they both had a passionate commitment to improving the life chances of inner city kids. They had a common interest at a very high level, but there was still a huge gap to convert that interest into a practical way forward. Being a teacher, Sarah did her homework before meeting the head teacher. She figured out they had three further common interests:

- She wanted to stay; the head needed her to stay. Attracting quality staff was time consuming, expensive and fraught with risk.
- She wanted more responsibility; the head had several programmes around behaviour management and a literacy drive which needed a team leader.
- She wanted to build her career and get a Master's degree: the head was under pressure to show the school governors what he was doing about professional development.

When they met, the head was mightily relieved to find that Sarah did not ask for the expected pay rise and promotion. It was a much more useful discussion about what she would do if she stayed. Eventually, they agreed that she would lead the literacy drive across the school, which would give her credits towards the Master's degree she was working on.

Finally, Sarah asked the head how he could help on pay and position. Too late, the head realised he had been put on the spot. He had to do something for Sarah. There was a long pause. He realised that with Sarah leading the literacy drive, that would save costs versus bringing in outside help.

Retaining Sarah would also save on the costs and risks of recruiting a replacement. Sarah was helping him save some precious budget: he could afford to share some of the savings with her. In the end Sarah got less than she had asked for, but more than she had expected. More important, both Sarah and the head left feeling that they had achieved a very satisfactory outcome. Neither had achieved their original position, but they had fulfilled their common interests.

Take a look at the classic positions outlined above, and you can normally find that a deeper interest lies behind each one, as follows:

Position	Example interests behind the position
I want a 25% pay rise	Can you help me maximise my long-term earnings potential?
Give me a 20% discount on this purchase	Can you minimise my cost of owning and using this product?
	Can you give me a story to make me look good when I tell my colleagues about this purchase?
Cut your budget 10% for next year	Can you help us meet next year's profit target better?
I want to be promoted	Can you help me progress my career?
I can't deliver this work before next week	Can you help me with my workload and priorities?

Once you find the interest behind the position, you have a chance of exploring more options. You no longer have a win–lose discussion. The potential for a win–win–win starts to emerge. People rarely volunteer these positions. Quite often they do not even know what their real interests are: they have become so fixated on winning a battle over price or something else that they have ignored the wider picture. You have to help them discover their real interests.

Once you do this you not only change the nature of the discussion: you change the nature of the relationship. You are no longer their adversary: you are their advisor. That is a far better position to be in.

There are two simple ways you can discover someone's real interests:

1 Do your homework. Most positions are reasonably predictable (I want a lower price, more bonus etc). And equally, the interests which lie behind the position are also fairly predictable. If you have prepared properly, you will be in a better position to use the next two discovery methods.

2 Offer some alternatives. Once you have done your homework, you should know what the typical alternatives are to the positions you are in. We will explore this further in the next section.

Win–lose discussions are natural, but unproductive. Influencers learn that winning allies is more important than winning arguments in the long term. When it comes to the next discussion, the loser in a win–lose discussion will be out for revenge. In contrast, the influencers have much easier rides to a win–win with their allies. Focusing on common interests rather than individual positions is the first step towards achieving a win–win.

> win–lose discussions are natural, but unproductive

Offer options

The typical 'position' discussion above is always a win–lose. There is nothing to bargain over except who gets the largest slice of the cake. But once you have got behind the stated position to someone's interests, you will find a range of options open up.

Position: win–lose	Example interests behind the position	Example options to explore
I want a 25% pay rise	Can you help me maximise my long-term earnings potential?	What are the long-term skills and experiences you need to maximise your value? What performance is required in the short term to show you are worth more? How much risk are you willing to take?
Give me a 20% discount on this purchase	Can you minimise my cost of owning and using this product? Can you give me a story to make me look good when I tell my colleagues about this purchase?	We can help you on financing, warranty, part exchange, minimising the cost of usage, product and service extras...
Cut your budget 10% for next year	Can you help us meet next year's profit target better?	How can I help you improve profit: pricing, volumes, costs, working capital? What risk will you take in market share, reducing headcount and skills etc?
I want to be promoted	Can you help me progress my career?	What skills do you want to grow? What experiences and assignments will help you most?
I can't deliver this work before next week	Can you help me with my workload and priorities?	What is the blockage and can we remove it? What are your other priorities and for who? Can we help by removing some of your other workload?

The win–lose becomes a win–win–win. The table above shows how the example win–lose positions in this chapter can be converted into interest and into options to explore.

The normal challenge in this discussion is that the person you are talking with has simply not thought of all the options. They have come in prepared for a negotiation which they want to win. Having put their boxing gloves on, they want to have the bout. To get to the options discussion you have to deploy two other key strategies of the effective influencer:

1 Listen: let them talk about their needs and wants.
2 Ask smart questions, as outlined above. Don't make smart statements and don't challenge them. If you do that, then they will put their boxing gloves back on and the bout will start.

Computing value: price versus package

I went to a store to buy a computer. The store manager and I did not have much of a common interest. The manager wanted to make as much money, and I wanted to spend as little money as possible for my new computer. I figured I had $1,000 to spend on the total package of hardware and software. It looked like we were going to have a head on collision over price.

But the store manager was smart. First, he took time to listen to what I wanted: good start. Then he suggested a computer which was below my budget: very smart. This showed I could trust him. He was not trying to escalate me into a higher price bracket. And then he confused me, which was really smart. He bamboozled me with choice.

First of all, there is a choice of computers and trade-offs around countless features: memory, speed, storage, graphics and much more. Even with a settled configuration, there is more choice: what software will be bundled; service and warranty guarantees; delivery and set up; financing (outright purchase versus leasing). The choice is bewildering. I now realised that focus on price was too simple: I needed to think harder about lifetime cost and value.

By the time I had worked through all the choices, my head was reeling. Fortunately, the sales manager made it easy for me. He reduced the choice back down to just two packages which seemed to suit me best: one at $25 a month for three years, the other at $35 a month. To make it easy for me, he threw in some extra software, an extra year of warranty and a data transfer package into the deal on the higher price package. He had offered me a concession, an apparent win. It was a concession which was standard practice, but it gave me the sense I was winning. I bought and was happy to have got a bargain…which had cost me more than I had originally budgeted.

By offering choice, the manager got away from the simple price discussion. It was now a price-value discussion. A price discussion is win–lose. Price–value can be a win–win discussion.

Many head on clashes can be avoided by changing the terms of the debate and offering options and alternatives. These alternatives will normally get away from haggling over positions to a richer discussion around interests, as outlined in the previous section. Typical examples of changing the terms of the debate include:

- from price to value
- from quantity to quality
- from inputs to outputs (the cost of soup labels to the profits of making soup)
- from job promotion to personal development.

Craft a story

Humans are risk averse. Risk aversion saved our ancestors from becoming breakfast for a brontosaurus. When we talk about risk, we normally think of rational risk: 'Will this product be defective?'

But the much bigger risk is personal and emotional: 'Will I look stupid if I make this decision?'

Even photocopiers are an emotional purchase. What on earth can be emotional about a photocopier? It should be a rational decision about copy speed, quality, reliability, overall cost and cost per sheet. Simple. Except that it is not that simple. If you are buying the photocopier for the office and it keeps on going wrong, you become the office idiot. Every time there is an urgent copy job which goes wrong, you get the blame. You are not just the office idiot, you are the office hate object. Suddenly, all the discussion about saving 0.1 pence per sheet of paper looks irrelevant.

As an exercise, think about the last time you purchased a mobile phone, or a car. Will you tell your friends and colleagues that you got a lousy deal and managed to get yourself ripped off? Or will you tell a story which shows that you got a pretty good deal and that you are a smart buyer and negotiator. Most humans like to show that they are smart. So what is the story that you will craft? There are plenty of ways you can show you got a good deal on that car you bought:

- great trade in price on the old car
- extended insurance or warranty
- free servicing period
- extra feature for free (alloy wheels, metallic paint etc)
- great financing deal.

Similarly with the mobile phone, there is plenty for everyone to brag about their phone in terms of features, price, performance and service. You can be reasonably sure that the sales person you were dealing with was not helping you as an act of charity: they will have got their bonus. But they will have helped you craft a story in your own mind about why you got a great deal. It is a story you probably use with friends and colleagues if ever asked about the deal you got.

Real estate agents can be expert at helping buyers craft a story to help themselves buy a property. One nearly convinced me to buy a complete wreck of a house. He had listened closely to what I wanted from a house, and I had failed to mention that it should not be a wreck. As we went from one horrendous space to another he was painting a picture in my mind of how one space could be the wonderful family room we wanted; another could be the study with great views and so on. By the time I left the property I no longer saw a wreck: I saw my ideal house. Fortunately, I signed nothing immediately and by the next day had woken up to realise that my dream house would be a nightmare renovation.

The emotional civil servants

We wanted to start a major new programme for a government department. We thought we had all the approvals and went to the final meeting with the government minister full of hope. The Minister turned us down flat inside three minutes and left the room. We were stunned. The programme appeared to tick every box and was certain to succeed. The civil servants told us that the programme was far too risky and could fail. Six months' work had just disappeared.

Later, we asked a few allies in the civil service what had really happened. Slowly, we pieced together the story. The first insight was that the job of a senior civil servant is not to act in the interests of the taxpayer or the country. If a civil servant values his or her career, then they know that their job is to protect their minister at all costs. Embarrassing your minister is a career limiting move. So the civil servants looked at our proposal and hated it.

The civil servants hated our proposal not because it might fail. They hated it because it might succeed. The more our programme succeeded, the more it would show that existing government programmes were a useless waste of taxpayers' money. And that would seriously embarrass the Minister. So the best thing to do with a good idea is to kill it.

Armed with this insight we went back to the civil servants. The obvious approach would be to address their rational concerns and show how our programme was a massive, guaranteed success. That would have been a suicide note for the programme. Instead, we showed how it would be a very modest programme; it would not interfere or compete with any of the existing programmes; of course, if it succeeded, it would be recognised as a personal success for the minister. The civil servants purred like a cat with the cream. We got our approval; it was a stunning success and the other government programmes were quietly killed. Successive ministers then proudly showed off how they had personally driven and sponsored our idea: we let them have their win.

We had gone behind the stated position of the civil servants, understood their real needs and the real risks they saw and finally we had crafted for them a story of how the programme would fit their needs perfectly. We had stopped promoting our idea and started to see the world through their eyes.

The art of crafting a story is to give the other person a win. Let them have something to brag about. The more options you can create, the more you will be able to find a way of letting them win something. Many of the options which a mobile phone seller or car salesman offer have low cost to them but high value to the buyer: they are easy wins to give. But the smart influencer does not make them appear easy. They give the concessions with the appearance of great regret: 'This is not normal at all...I will have to ask my manager... never done this before...but in your case...' The more reluctant you appear, the more the other side will be convinced that they have achieved a great coup. You are quietly flattering their ego. You are giving a story they will value: 'I am a smart sort of person...'

Agree in public, argue in private

As soon as someone says something in public, they are committed. They can not unwind their position without loss of face. Notice how politicians go through yoga-like contortions to avoid changing a public position, even when any sane view of their situation would demand a change. In the workplace, as soon as someone says 'that won't work...' they are committed: they will then find more or less any reason to justify their initial instinct.

For the purposes of influencing, the critical distinction is between public and private. Any meeting where there are more than two people present is public. The introducing a third person means that discussion is no longer in confidence.

> any meeting where there are more than two people present is public

For this reason, most influencing happens quietly behind closed doors and a one-to-one basis. The purpose of a meeting, for an influencer, is never to make a decision. The value of a public meeting (with more than two people present) is to give public confirmation to all the deals that have been struck in private. Each person around the table wants the comfort of knowing that they are not alone in supporting your brilliant or crazy idea. Collective agreement is important: if everyone agrees then no one can be singled out if things go wrong later on.

If there is one person who can not be influenced in private, then at least the private discussions allow you to do three things which help:

1 You understand why the person disagrees: you can narrow the disagreement down to one or two highly specific issues.

2 You build up a coalition of support which isolates the person who disagrees: once they see the power of the coalition they will normally back down, having made their various points.

3 You have followed fair process: you have given the individual a chance to be heard. This show of respect will draw much of the sting and venom out of the opposition.

Keep doubts and opposition private; make agreements public.

Summary

Win–win–win is about mindset and creativity.

The win–win–win mindset depends on seeing the world through the eyes of the person you wish to influence. You can not offer them a win unless you know what a win looks like for them. And the good news is that the win for them is about perception as much as reality. Find a concession, an offer which will make them look good in their own eyes and in the eyes of their peers.

To find the win–win–win requires creativity. Creativity can come from innate genius on the spur of the moment and some of it can come from experience. A more reliable way of being creative is to work as a team. Prepare sales calls, negotiations and important meetings with the help of your team. The more you discuss it, the more options, potential concessions and win–wins will appear. You will gain more insight into how the other party thinks. Spontaneity is best when it is well rehearsed.

The win–lose mindset can win today's battle. But it makes it much harder to win tomorrow's battle: the loser will be twice as resistant next time around. The win–win–win allows you to win without fighting today. It then makes it even easier to win again next time, because you have an ally, not an enemy.

Chapter 6
Give to take

Generosity is a scarce commodity. As business grows harder and meaner, generosity becomes ever scarcer. As generosity becomes scarcer, it becomes more valuable. This is good news for influencers. A little generosity goes a long way: it is easy to stand out from the crowd of more self-interested colleagues. Influencers take a longer-term perspective: generosity is all about self-interest in the long term. It helps build willing partners, supporters and allies.

There are two sorts of generosity. The most common sort of generosity builds popularity. There is another sort of generosity which builds influence and power. We need to know which is which.

To understand generosity as popularity we need to look at Sue's story. Sue was, by some distance, the most popular PA on the executive floor. Everyone would stop to talk to her, from the mail man to the CEO. She always had a ready smile and easy banter. She also always had a large bowl of sweets by her desk and had a habit of bringing in cakes to celebrate birthdays, weddings, holidays, Fridays: any excuse would do. Looking at her, it appeared that she was often the main beneficiary of her largesse, but that was all part of her character and appeal. After about a year, her boss was moved to another division: both Sue and the boss agreed that it was not the right thing for her to make the move as well. In the subsequent reorganisation, disaster struck. No one wanted to have Sue as their PA. She may have been popular, but she was not a very good PA. She left to spread her goodwill and smiles elsewhere. It was a sad parting for everyone involved, which they tried to celebrate with a final cake in the office.

Sue was, without question, generous and popular. But she was clearly not influential or powerful. Cakes, sweets and gossip are not the route to influence for any manager. For managers, generosity has to take another form.

Politicians consistently fall into Sue's trap. They crave popularity but lose respect. They bribe us with our own money. Instead of handing out sweets, they hand out tax breaks, subsidies and favourable legislation to every pressure group. They make half promises and try to be friends with everyone. The search for popularity leads to weakness: they find it hard to say no to anyone. Worse, it leads to the loss of trust and respect. People who receive the politician's sweets think it is their entitlement and ask for more; people who get no sweets get angry. And as the cost of the politician's largesse grows, and the broken half promises stack up, so the credibility of the politician erodes. Generosity is a good way to temporary popularity, but it can destroy long-term credibility and influence. Generosity has to be managed well to work.

Influential generosity is marked out by four characteristics. It should be:

1 Customised, not generic.

2 Earned, not unearned.

3 Measured, not unlimited.

4 Requested, not unrequested.

As we shall see, these principles count because they maximise the chances of the generosity being valued and reciprocated. If generosity is neither valued nor reciprocated, we may find ourselves wearing Sue's shoes: we become popular but dispensable. If we follow the right principles, we can acquire allies and supporters who will help us when we need help.

One example will show how to be generous effectively. A senior manager wanted me to move into her department. I did not know her well, although she appeared to be doing interesting work. I had other commitments and was not very interested in listening to her overtures. Eventually, she persuaded me to do a small presentation to her team on my current work. It was a chance to show off; it was easy to do and I was allowed to pick the time and place for the presentation. Easy give. And I was being set up without knowing it.

At the presentation everyone was very kind and flattering. They at least pretended to look interested and impressed. A few days later, a bottle of fancy champagne arrived on my desk: the senior manager had done her homework and had even found out which brand I liked most. I rarely bought it because it was so expensive. It was a gift which scored a bull's eye on three of the four principles of generosity:

- It was highly customised to my interests and needs: it showed that she cared. My existing boss had no clue what I liked or did not like, and did not seem to care.

- The gift felt like it had been earned, and so I valued it. It was not just a gift: it was recognition of work well done, and recognition is always welcome. Recognition seemed to be a foreign land to my current boss.

- It was a measured gift: she did not shower me with presents. That would have been crude bribery. This was much more subtle bribery. It set the expectation that I could not get something for nothing: rewards had to be earned.

She then asked me for another favour, helping her on an existing project. I helped and was given more recognition. She had set up the process of give and take. Incrementally, I was being committed to her and split from my existing boss. After a couple of months I willingly made the switch.

Give to take is a powerful way of building commitment. Let's see how the four principles of give to take can be applied in practice.

1 Customised, not generic, generosity

Generosity pays when it is customised. The free pen which everyone gets at a conference has low value: the pen which is presented to you as an award for outstanding service has much higher value.

generosity pays when it is customised

A global partner's meeting showed how generosity works or fails depending on how customised it is. There were over 1,000 of us in a huge conference hall. It felt like a plenary session of the old Soviet communist party: all the comrades were expected to raise their hands and approve the decisions of other comrades, proving that neither partners nor comrades are ever truly equal. Managing the show was a huge effort. Deep in the bowels of the building there was a troupe of harried secretaries sorting out all the last minute crises. Inevitably, they had an endless stream of pompous partners passing their way demanding immediate resolution of vexatious logistics, communications and other problems. I could see their hearts sink when I approached: they saw another problem looming. I went in and thanked them for all their thankless work. They waited for the real reason for my visit, the impossible request I was going to make. There was no ulterior motive. I just thanked them. I left them dumbstruck. Back in the office, I suddenly found all the secretaries being unusually helpful: hard to meet executives suddenly had free space in their diaries, life became easy. I later learned that I was the only one of over 1,000 partners who had bothered to recognise them and thank them for their effort.

At the end of the same meeting the CEO (senior partner) summoned the organising secretaries on stage, thanked them and gave them all bouquets of flowers. It was a case study in how not to be generous. Far from being grateful, the secretaries were embarrassed and annoyed. The CEO's gesture failed because:

- It was generic generosity. There was no thought about what the staff might want. They got flowers at the end of every conference, even though they could not fly home with them. There were many gifts the staff might have wanted: the CEO did not know what they wanted, and did not even know most of their names. Generic generosity appears synthetic and insincere.

- The staff had been told to buy their own flowers and put them on expenses. They then handed the flowers to the CEO offstage. He walked on stage and handed the flowers right back to them. There was no hint of personal generosity or effort about the gift. Again, it failed to pass the test of being personal and customised.

- It was ritual. It was what happened at the end of every conference. It failed the test of being unexpected. Further, the ritual simply served to embarrass the staff who preferred not to be paraded on stage like some curious exhibit.

Effective generosity is customised both to the giver and the taker. A mentoring relationship is the classic form of customised generosity because:

- The mentor is giving up personal time and effort.
- The mentor is focused completely on the specific needs of the person asking for advice.

For example, when I first stumbled into the world of consulting I had no idea what I was doing. The wags will argue that nothing has changed. There were three founding partners. All were formidable intellects. One of them liked to eat analysts and junior consultants for breakfast. He was brilliant, but terrifying. He also found it very hard to get any staff for his projects: no one could meet his standards, and no one wanted to work for him. No one wanted to be his breakfast. He ended up working himself into an early grave. The other two were just as sharp, but they always seemed to have time for people. They did not boss, they did not humiliate. They listened, supported and helped. They were generous with the one thing that busy people really do not have enough of: their own time. As a result, everyone wanted to work with them and for them. They were time generous not only with staff, but with clients. They were always prepared to listen, help and support a struggling client. It was all part of the service, regardless of whether there was a paid assignment or not.

Staff and clients flocked to these two partners. They came to rely on their generous, wise and committed support. Not surprisingly, this turned out to be a success formula. Clients have remained with them for 20 years or more; staff remain loyal over decades. Staff and clients who abused their generosity fell by the wayside. Freeloaders found it harder to open the partners' diaries. But there are many more who have been very happy to reciprocate. Clients always turn to these two partners when there is paid work to be done, and staff are always willing to work on projects led by the two partners.

Generosity is not just about chocolates and champagne. These things have monetary value, but not necessarily personal value. The most precious resources in an organisation tend to be things like time and recognition. When you give people your time, you are investing your most precious and limited resource in them: people respond to that vote of confidence. When you give them recognition, that is also a vote of confidence in them. Once you have made the investment, you can expect to ask for a return on that investment: most people will give willingly. You have set up the process of give to take.

2 Earned, not unearned, generosity

If you go into a senior banker's office, it is not uncommon to see it full of tombstones. These are not the product of some weird fetish involving graveyards: even bankers have not fallen that far, yet. The tombstones are little Perspex mementoes that are shaped like tombstones. They enclose a piece of paper which records various financing deals they have put in place and have been announced in the financial press. The value of each tombstone can be measured in pennies, and yet rich bankers display them proudly as valuable trophies. The trophies are valued because they represent hard won triumphs and are a record of their achievement. They have pride of place in the office. If you gave the same banker a nicely designed Perspex paperweight with your company logo on it, the banker would probably put it straight into the number 1 file: the waste basket.

As a general rule, we value what we earn more than what is free. In running a sales force I found salesmen would compete viciously to win the monthly prize, which would often be pretty much a token: perhaps a nice pen or a dinner out. At the annual conference the salesmen would be inundated with free pens and meals:

> we value what we earn more than what is free

they were worthless. The conference pen lacks meaning or value. The monthly prize may have modest financial value, but has huge symbolic value. It shows who is top dog for the month. It is very public recognition for achievement.

If you are going to give for free, give well. If you give and do a shoddy job, people will remember the shoddy job rather than your generosity. You will lose influence rather than gain it. For instance, when we started Teach First the government leaned on a very prestigious advertising agency to give us some free support in developing our advertising. The agency clearly hated doing this: they wanted to make money, not spend it. But to keep government contracts they felt they had to help us. So they did the minimum required and were clearly not interested. Their work was rubbish. Even though they were free, we fired them. Our implied message to them was 'you are worth less than nothing', which is not good for a top advertising agency. Despite having close to no money, we hired a small agency which did a stellar job for us because they saw their chance to make their name with us.

In contrast, McKinsey did some free consulting for Teach First when we started. And they were truly outstanding. They did not treat us as an impoverished start up, as second-class citizens. They did top-class work; they made introductions for us; they let us use their offices for recruiting the initial team and initial participants. They have since then been active partners and have hopefully shared in some of the profile Teach First has achieved with top politicians of all parties. By doing good work they built influence; by doing poor work the advertising agency lost influence.

If you give, give your best.

3 Measured, not unlimited, generosity

Giving your best is true in terms of quality, but not in terms of quantity.

The more you give, the less it will be valued. For this, think of Mars bars. If you give one to a child to eat, the child will be happy. The second will also be quickly accepted. The greedier children may be able to get through the third Mars bar. By the time the child is confronted with the fourth, fifth or sixth Mars bar, they will be groaning. The seventh Mars bar will be as welcome as the plague. Be measured in your generosity. What is scarce is more valued than what is abundant. Diamonds and coal are both carbon: scarcity dictates which is more prized.

> the more you give, the less it will be valued

If we give and continue to give unconditionally, we can quickly become exploited. I helped one charity and they started asking for more and more help which I was happy to give. Eventually, they were consuming half my time and I was being asked to do things which they could have done by hiring someone on minimum wage. I had simply become free labour to be used whenever they could not be bothered to do something themselves. I told them I would do 2–3 days a month in future: suddenly, they worked out how to use me to get most value out of me.

Clearly, there is a balance to be struck. If you give too much, you will be taken for granted and exploited. If you only give in return for something, then that is not generosity: that is trading. The key is timing. Be generous early. First impressions count. Early acts of generosity mark your character. Do not ask, or even expect, anything in return for a while. If you ask for something back, you have become a trader and you have ceased to be generous.

Over time it will become clear who are freeloaders that want to exploit you, and who are prepared to reciprocate. You do not need to argue or complain to the freeloaders. As your flow of generosity dries up, they will quietly disappear. You can focus on those people with whom you can build a more productive relationship.

Measured generosity requires clarity about who to help, how to help and how much to help. That means learning to say no to requests for help. This can feel awkward. But it is far better to say no than commit to doing something and doing it poorly. Poor work destroys personal credibility, even if it was done generously out of your discretionary time and effort. Only agree to help if you have the relevant capability (skill), capacity (time) and will (you want to help). 'No' may be hard to say, but saves tears later. There are three principles to saying no gracefully:

1 Be clear about your decision: lack of clarity leads to disaster and mismatched expectations later. If you appear unreliable you lose credibility, trustworthiness and influence.

2 Be clear and honest about why you can not do it: most people will respect your decision if they understand why you are making it. If you lack the capability or capacity to help, say so.

3 If possible, offer an alternative. Perhaps you can help later, or someone else may be more expert, or you may be able to help with just part of the problem. Offering an alternative at least shows some goodwill.

4 Requested, not unrequested, help

There is a phrase which sends a chill down the spine of any practising manager: 'Hello. We're from Head Office and we are here to help you.' This is the sort of help which has your finances, operations and staff being turned upside down and inside out. Imposed help is rarely helpful. It is interference, not help.

Despite this, unrequested help flourishes. Managers help their teams with unwanted reviews, coaching, advice and direction. Colleagues help each other with advice. This can be lethal. In the executive suite there is an informal no pissing rule: 'I will not piss on your territory if you do not piss on mine.' This means that meetings of the executive team are a bizarre ritual in which there are a series of one to one duels between the CEO and each director. All the other directors get to watch the show until it is their turn for a duel with the CEO. Advice may be well meant, but it is treated as interference. In the executive suite that is called politics and nearly always results in retaliation.

The only help people value is the help they ask for. If they don't ask, don't give. It can be difficult to resist the temptation, especially if you see a team member struggling or going in the wrong direction. Let them learn: they will learn more from experience than from some unasked for interference, however well meaning it is. If they are too shy or too proud to ask for help, an innocent 'how's it going?' as you pass their desk should be enough to prompt the request.

Summary

Generosity is the art of taking by giving. It is not like being Father Christmas and distributing presents in the pursuit of popularity. Leaders do not need to be popular. They need to be trusted and respected. The search for popularity leads to weakness and a cycle of ever growing expectations. Building trust builds commitment and loyalty which are much less fickle than the demands of popularity.

Generosity in the management world is about giving the most scarce resource of all. The most scarce resource in management is not money, it is time. Being generous with personal time appears to be suicidal when there are so many day to day pressures to meet. But by creating a network of alliances, mutual obligations and debts which can be called in, the influencer invests heavily in the future. It is an investment which saves time and raises performance in the longer term.

> the most scarce resource in management is not money, it is time

Ultimately, generosity is a habit. Fortunately, it is a habit that can be acquired. It is not just profitable to give, it is also enjoyable. And the meaner business becomes, the easier it is for the selfless and generous manager to stand out and become influential.

Chapter 7

Play the right tune

Ever since Freud and his disciple Jung created psychotherapy, therapists have been trying to figure out how people work. How much progress they have made is open to debate. Most of us do not have the time, expertise or need to become psychotherapists. We need some short hand methods of quickly understanding and influencing our friends and colleagues.

Fortunately, we do not need to put our colleagues on the couch to understand them. To get onto their wavelength, there are two things we can do.

1 Write the right script.

2 Tune into our colleagues: adapt to their style.

For each of these goals, there is a simple tool we can use to help ourselves.

Write the right script

I recently became a trillionaire, many times over. In real hard cash. I reckon I have $400,000,000,000,000. I may be out by the odd billion, but in truth we trillionaires are not too bothered by a few billion dollars here or there. I have the money in my pocket. Unfortunately, the dollars are Zimbabwean dollars and my four $100 trillion notes are not enough to buy me a bus fare in Zimbabwe, the land of the world's starving billionaires.

Gideon Gono has been the governor of the Central Bank of Zimbabwe since 2003. In that time, Zimbabwe has slid from being the prosperous bread basket of Africa, to hyperinflation, mass unemployment and dependency on food aid. As the top central banker of a Zimbabwe what sort of story do you construct for yourself:

a   I have been a complete idiot who has destroyed a prosperous country through a combination of greed, corruption and incompetence, or

b   I have brilliantly withstood hostile foreign sanctions and introduced innovative policies which the rest of the world now follows, which shows that God is on my side.

You would probably construct a positive story about yourself. This is what Gideon Gono has done. Here is what he said to *Newsweek* in January 2009: 'I found myself doing extraordinary things that aren't in the textbooks. Then the IMF asked the U.S. to please print money. I began to see the whole world now in a mode of practicing what they have been saying I should not. I decided that God had been on my side and had come to vindicate me.'

Now think about who he listens to and who influences him. Will it be people who challenge his world view and tell him he is an idiot, or will it be people who support his world view? The chances are that he listens to people who understand and respect his script. If you want to understand people, understand their personal script or self-image. Everyone has a personal script, and they tend to be positive scripts.

90% of people think they are above average. This is statistically impossible but emotionally inevitable

As a test, rate yourself on the following activities as either below or above average relative to the rest of humanity: honesty, reliability, trustworthiness, driving, working and loving. Typically, 90% of people think they are above average. This is statistically impossible but emotionally inevitable. This picture is reflected in the annual assessment ritual. In many firms, 90% of people are rated as average or above. The remaining 10% either move on, shape up or get fired. It is human nature to think well of ourselves.

Repeated studies show that the superiority delusion is alive and well. A 1976 College Board study asked 829,000 US students about their ability to get on with others. 100% of them thought they were above average. A quarter of the students thought they were in the top 1% of people able to get on with others. These are the people who are running the nation and its major businesses today.

Similarly, in 2000, 87% of Stanford MBA students thought they were above the average of their peers at Stanford. That matters because it leads to bad career choices. Typically, about one in ten people joining a top consulting firm or investment bank will reach partner level or equivalent. With all the students suffering the superiority syndrome, they are all convinced that they will be the one in ten. Most of them will discover that they were wrong.

In a study of US drivers, 93% of them thought they were above average in terms of skill. See what happens after an accident: everyone believes they are the good driver and the other person is an idiot. We also tend to think that the world fails to recognise our innate superiority. This paves the way for one of the great and simple influencing techniques, flattery. If you recognise someone's innate superiority, which no one else seems to have noticed, you will quickly win an ally. Flattery is covered in more detail in Chapter 12.

Our individual scripts are much richer than deluding ourselves into believing our own superiority over everyone else. Our scripts are about who we are and how we are.

Once you understand people's self-image, you can make them do more or less anything, provided it reinforces that self-image.

For instance, one boss had me worked out completely. He knew I was an adventurer: I loved challenge and excitement. My boss also had a problem. The Japan business was not so much the land of the rising sun: it was more the land of the sinking business. It was a bottomless pit of endless losses. He needed someone to turn it around. My boss gave me a five-minute pitch about the excitement, exotic adventure and challenge of Japan and I was hooked. There were some minor problems: I spoke no Japanese, had never been to Japan and was completely unqualified for the task. And I was offered only a one-way ticket: that made it even more exciting. If I had thought about it, I would have turned it down: but logic was overwhelmed by emotion. Not going would be a denial of how I saw myself and who I was: it was impossible for me not to accept the lousy challenge for the next three years of my life.

It takes time and effort to decode other people. But once you have made the investment, it keeps on paying dividends. Understanding people's self-image is the key to decoding people.

> understanding people's self-image is the key to decoding people

We all have a self-image of who we are. It may or may not be how other people see us. Our self-image can often be captured in a simple story about who we are and how we relate to the rest of the world. Inevitably, every story is unique because every human is unique. But in the workplace we can spot some common stories about how people like to see themselves. Listed below are ten of the most common archetypes that you can see at work. As you skim through the list, you will probably find a few of your colleagues who fit into some of these archetypes. Other colleagues may be a combination of archetypes, or you may be able to create your own script for them.

Once you understand how colleagues see themselves, you can work out three more things:

1 How to use them: what value they bring.

2 How not to use them: where they are a liability.

3 How to influence them sustainably.

For all of the archetypes below, there is a very brief sketch of each of these three things.

Workplace archetypes

Winner

Script: 'I win at *everything*: jobs, love, money, driving, sport, investing'

Style: Highly competitive, driven to over-achieve, high need for control

Value: Point them at the right windmill and they will charge

Downside: Divisive. Poor in adversity: delusional and often self-destructive

Influencing key: Show you are also a winner, in another area. Do not compete directly, but do not be submissive: winners like to work with non-competing winners.

Angel

Script: 'I am an island of compassion and help in a cruel and heartless world'

Style: Caring, nurturing and supportive

Value: Can be a calming and unifying force in adverse circumstances

Downside: More focused on dealing with people than dealing with tasks

Influencing key: Be empathetic, admire their work and ask for their help. They will like nurturing you.

Craftsman/technocrat

Script: 'I am highly professional and skilled in my chosen trade'

Style: Highly rational and analytical; not great on tasks or people

Value: Often good at what they do

Downside: Rarely make good managers; tend to be insular and focused on their own job

Influencing key: Respect, recognise their expertise: do not question their talent. Contradiction often works: 'This looks impossible, I was told no one in your department can do this...' They will then prove you wrong by doing the impossible, thank you.

Puritan

Script: 'I am an island of decency in an ocean of immorality and idleness'

Style: Decency, honesty, fair play, hard work

Value: Often reliable team members who will work hard and quietly to deliver

Downside: Don't invite them to your party, and don't mention your latest expenses claim

Influencing key: Listen and let them moralise. Empathise with them. Recognise their work and their values, which may well be overlooked by other people.

Aristocrat

Script: 'I am socially superior and very well connected: should I talk to you?'

Style: Highly aware of people and status

Value: Often well connected within and beyond the firm: can open doors

Downside: Toxic to the values of your organisation

Influencing key: Very pliable if you can offer them access to prestigious events and people. They want the bragging rights. Make them sweat: do not give them what they want immediately.

Bureaucrat

Script: 'I am diligent, effective and largely unrecognised'

Style: Guided by the twin stars of fairness and efficiency, on a good day.

Value: Reliable, especially for administrative tasks

Downside: Focus on process, not outcomes. Slow, uncreative, risk averse. May think management is about procedures, not people.

Influencing key: Show respect, comply with rules and procedures: avoid risk. Be clear and detailed about what you need from them.

Hero

Script: 'I save the world/firm/project from imminent disaster'

Value: Often good in crises and with tight deadlines. Will make things happen.

Downside: Can be drama queens

Influencing key: Respect, admire their role in saving the world. Show you need them to save the world again in your area, and that this time the world will recognise it and be grateful.

Policeman

Script: 'My job is to stop disaster happening: I am the sheriff who controls all the cowboys around here'

Value: Can identify and avoid risk: may be found in legal, health & safety, audit, brand police etc

Downside: Brains hard wired to say no

Influencing key: Involve them early. This shows them respect and means that their comments can be incorporated early and painlessly. Leave it late and you have an expensive political struggle.

Intellectual

Script: 'I am smarter than the fools who are my bosses and colleagues'

Value: Driven by intellectual challenges

Downside: Not good at people; can be a loner

Influence key: Recognise their brilliance, ask for their advice, wisdom and experience. Give them a platform to display their talent.

Victim

Script: 'I suffer the slings and arrows of outrageous fortune with courage and fortitude. Poor me'

Value: Not much. Believes events control them, rather than them controlling events

Downside: Achieves little; drain on enthusiasm; passive victim

Influencing key: Best to avoid. If necessary, listen and empathise.

There are four common themes in dealing with all of these scripts:

- Listen to people: let them talk about themselves. That is how you will discover their script or self-image. You will be learning the tune to play to them.

- Respect their world view, empathise but do not try to compete with them. Do not try to be a better winner/victim/craftsman than the person you are talking to. They want to be exceptional. Do not challenge or threaten their world view: they will become highly defensive. Let them live with their own version of reality, even if you do not believe their nonsense. Your job is not to challenge or change their world view. You need to influence them, which means working with them, not against them.

- Recognise them. Very few people think that they are over-recognised. Most of us suspect that our talents and achievements are not adequately recognised in the wider world. Use this to your advantage. Recognise them in private, of course. But you may be able to go further. Perhaps you can stage an opportunity at an offsite meeting, at a presentation, at a dinner or awards event where they can be showcased.

- Money is not the main motivator. Money recognises their value relative to their colleagues. Even $1 million is an insult if their colleague is given more. As a colleague, you probably do not control their pay anyway, so you can focus on other influencing tools. Remember, no one denies who they are: if your idea or request reinforces their self-image, they will find it extremely hard to deny your request.

Two examples will show how you can use people's scripts to influence:

Amy was terrified at the prospect of presenting to the board, who were at least three levels above her. She did not know any of them and she feared it would make or break her career. She did not want to do it. Outside work, Amy was a different character. She was an enthusiastic member of several community groups including a theatre group. She had given herself two scripts: at work she was the junior manager still learning her trade and working in the back room of the business. In her social life she was the organiser and performer who liked to be centre stage. She needed to move her social script to work. So she was offered some presentation training, which would be run by an actor. The simple message was that all presentations are a performance: acting helps presenting. The presentation training would also help her acting. Eventually she went to the board, but she did not present: she performed for the board and performed brilliantly.

Dan was very clever and very cynical. He was the classic techno-crat: brilliant with his statistics but pretty much unable to relate to other human beings. He had a fairly dysfunctional script where he was the unrecognised and undervalued expert who knew all the answers, but no one was prepared to listen. He could do outstanding analysis, but he could also do highly destructive analysis: he could demolish more or less any spreadsheet or financial analysis which was presented to him.

For a big proposal, we knew we needed him on side because top management would use him to screen our proposal. The normal script would involve us having a long and bloody battle with him, interspersed with occasional pleas for a truce. Instead, we decided not to present the proposal to him. We went and listened to him and heard about the projects he was working on. We picked one which sounded relevant and made ourselves enthusiastic about it. We said that his work was so interesting, could he present a paper on it at our annual conference? We told him more people needed to hear about his work. Dan was delighted. At last he was getting recognition for his work; he was being given a platform to display his skills. It would be extra work, but it was well worth it.

Later, we went along and asked for some more help. Finally, we told him we needed some help on a proposal for top management. Dan the clever cynic suddenly became Dan the enthusiastic supporter. He showed us how our proposal was deeply flawed (he could have torn it to shreds) and then went on to show how we could make it bullet proof. We had taken the simple step of recognising and valuing an under-recognised and undervalued technocrat. So instead of fighting against us, he started fighting for us.

The dark side and the bright side of the script

There is a dark side to working the script. It can be highly manipulative and potentially destructive. At an extreme, the 'martyrdom' videos of suicide bombers show that they have completely bought into a script which tells them that the best thing a human can do is to kill other humans randomly. All dictators have a script that tells them that what they are doing is good. Often they assume that they do not represent the nation: they *are* the nation. If they are the nation, then all opposition is by definition sedition and treachery, and also all of the resources of the nation belong to them: wealth, power and corruption all go hand in hand.

At a more mundane level, British Members of Parliament have been found fleecing the taxpayer for personal gain: they have been caught putting all sorts of things on expenses from the cost of having their moat cleared to buying a floating duck house. And it is not one or two politicians who have had their snouts in the trough: it looks that the majority have been in the swill. These are not obviously corrupt people. For the most part, they got into politics to change the world, not to buy a duck house. So what went wrong? Collectively they wrote the wrong script which goes something like this:

'Every day we meet rich and powerful people. We work harder than most of them and are more deserving, but our salaries are small compared to the people we meet. Public opinion will not let us pay ourselves more, but we can make it up through the expenses system. As long as we stick within the rules (script) we have set for ourselves, then the expenses are a discrete way of making up our salaries.'

This script was self-reinforcing. When some politicians started following the script, initially without criticism, it showed that the script was a good one. Other politicians followed until it became standard practice. Internally, their script made perfect sense to themselves, until the details were exposed to public scrutiny. Then it looked like total folly and an abuse of taxpayers' money and trust.

When someone's script goes wrong, the consequences are ugly. Zinedine Zidane, captain of the French football team was playing in the World Cup final, a match watched by over a billion people. Zidane was already a winner: he had won the World Cup before. He had a winner's script in his head. This was going to be his moment when he led his country once again to inevitable victory over Italy, their opposition. Unfortunately, the script started to go wrong. Italy were winning and time was running out. Someone had stolen his script. He was not a winner any more. If he was not a winner, he was nothing: he had no other script. He was not just losing a match, he was losing everything he stood for and his whole self-image. With a little Italian provocation, Zidane lost the plot completely and headbutted an opponent. He was sent off, France were down to ten men and were condemned to defeat by his moment of madness.

As with all forms of power, influence can be put to good use or poor use. Influence is amoral: it makes no value judgements about what is right or wrong. Used well, scripts can not only help influence other people: we can also help ourselves by writing the right script for ourselves.

A few examples will show how we can change our life chances by changing our script.

Teach First puts outstanding teachers into challenging inner city schools. Many of the kids who attend these schools inherit very low aspirations from their parents and their life horizons are limited. Their script is of low ambition and has negative expectations. One Teach First initiative took 100 such children on visits to universities. Raising expectations and showing them what was possible helped the children begin to change their life script. The future was no longer about joining a gang or working in the local supermarket. They saw what was possible with hard work; 90% of them went on to university, and several of them went to elite universities.

Professor Richard Wiseman, in his book *The Luck Factor*, shows what makes people lucky. Part of it is that they make their own luck. The other part of it is that they create an internal script in which they see themselves as lucky. As a result they tend to recall all the moments when they got lucky. Unlucky people recall all the times they got unlucky. On the same trip, the lucky driver will recall all the times the lights changed in his favour. His unlucky passenger sitting next to him will recall all the times the lights changed against them. The same experience can be lucky or unlucky depending on the script you choose.

If we use scripts well, we can not only influence others positively, we can also influence our own life. What's your script, and what do you want it to be?

Understanding and adapting to the style of our colleagues

There is a whole cottage industry devoted to understanding the styles of different people. For the most part, this involves categorising people and putting them in neat little boxes: people should not be put in boxes until they are dead.

Perhaps the most famous of these systems is MB/TI (the Myers-Briggs Type Indicators). MB/TI offers a series of style or type trade-offs. You can be:

> people should not be put in boxes until they are dead

- Extrovert or Introvert (E or I)
- Sensing or Intuitive (S or N)
- Thinking or Feeling (T or F)
- Judging or Perceiving (J or P).

MB/TI assigns each person a style and an acronym such as ESTJ or INFP. It provides insight, but it is difficult to learn and harder to apply. A short, revisionist and unauthorised version of how MB/TI works is shown below:

A REVISIONIST VERSION OF MB/TI

Type	Description	Positive impact	Negative impact
Extroversion (E)	Gains energy from others Speaks then thinks	Spreads energy, enthusiasm	Loud mouth, does not include other people
Introversion (I)	Gains energy from within, thinks before speaks	Thoughtful, gives space to others	Nothing worth saying? Uneasy networker
Sensing (S)	Observes outside world More facts, less ideas	Practical, concrete, detailed	Dull, unimaginative
Intuitive (N)	Pays attention to self, inner world, ideas	Creative, imaginative	Flighty, impractical, unrealistic
Thinking (T)	Decides with the head and logic	Logical, rational, intellectual	Cold and heartless
Feeling (F)	Listens to the heart	Empathetic, understanding	Soft headed, fuzzy thinker, bleeding heart
Judging (J)	Organised, scheduled, tidy	High work ethic, focused and reliable	Compulsive neat freak, Uptight, rigid, rule bound
Perceiving (P)	Keeps options open, opportunistic	Work–life balance, enjoys work	Lazy, messy, aimless and unreliable

Previously published in Owen, J (2012) *Leadership Skills Handbook*,
2nd edn, Kogan Page, London

As you look at the positive impact of each style, you are only human if you assume you have the positive virtues of every style. In practice, you are meant to be either extrovert or introvert, sensing or intuitive, thinking or feeling, judging or perceiving. You have to choose between the styles. A quicker way to make your choice is to look at the negative impacts of each style. This allows you to identify your own style and that of your partner relatively quickly. If you spend a day or two in seminars about MB/TI (or any of the other style tools) you will discover their richness and depth. It takes months to become an expert practitioner. This defeats the object of the exercise: we do not want to become psychology experts. We need some simple short hand for understanding and influencing our colleagues.

There are many other personality tests out there. Each claims to be better than the others. Quite a few are available on the web, if you want to while away an odd hour getting to know who you are. To use them, most of these tools require months or even years of training, and they also often require detailed analysis of each of your colleagues. Managers do not have time to become psycho-therapists, nor do they have the time to analyse each of their colleagues in detail. We need something simpler, and quicker: welcome to the style compass.

The style compass

The easiest way to start is to think about how the person you want to influence operates. Forget the psychological mumbo jumbo. Just focus on the sorts of behaviour that you see most consistently. There are all sorts of possible trade-offs and behaviours you could identify. Here are a few to start with:

- Big picture vs. Detail
- Email vs. Face to face
- Task focus vs. People focus
- Open vs. Defensive
- Controlling vs. Empowering
- Analysing vs. Action
- Risk taking vs. Risk avoiding
- Outcomes vs. Process

- Inductive vs. Deductive
- Prompt vs. Tardy
- Quick vs. Slow
- Positive vs. Cynical
- Judging vs. Sensing
- Rash vs. Contemplative
- Morning vs. Afternoon
- Written vs. Spoken word
- Numbers vs. Words.

Do not go through all of these behaviours and try to categorise your colleague on all of the trade-offs. Just think of the four main characteristics of how the person behaves. For example, one manic chief executive I worked with had a very short attention span and very short temper. Monday mornings were the worst: he wound himself up like a demented toy soldier over the weekend, and would come in spraying orders and commands everywhere. By Friday afternoon he would have wound down and become calmer and more reflective, especially as most of his colleagues left early on Fridays. So how could I influence him positively? Easy: hang around late on Friday and have a nice informal chat with him when he was calm and not distracted. This was weak on theory, strong in practice. There is no formal psychological analysis tool that would lead you to this insight; a little observation works where a lot of theory fails.

Once you have identified the main behaviours and style of the colleague you want to influence, map them out on a style compass as shown in Figure 7.1. For each characteristic you have identified, there is probably an opposite. So in the example below, my colleague is cautious, likes detail, is facts focused and is best in the morning. The opposite of this would be someone who is risk taking, big picture and people focused.

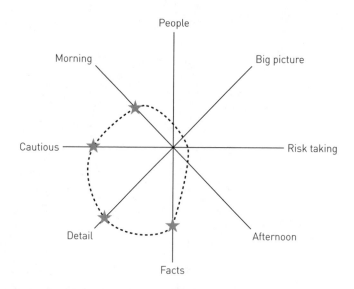

Figure 7.1 Style compass of my colleague

The style compass gives you a visual map of what this colleague is like. Now you have mapped your colleague, map yourself against the same criteria. Even if other criteria are far more important in shaping your behaviour, ignore them. Your focus is on your colleague's style, not on yourself. You need to see yourself through their eyes, not your eyes. You may overlap completely: in this case you may naturally get on very well together. Or, in the example shown in Figure 7.2, you may find that you look very different from your colleague.

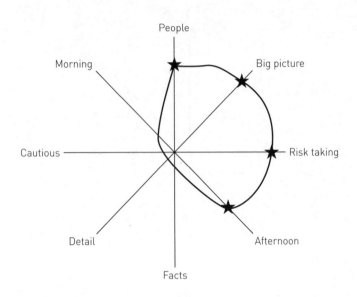

Figure 7.2 My style compass

Once you have mapped yourself and your colleague, you can take the next obvious step: combine the two style compasses to see how you compare (Figure 7.3). In this case, me and my colleague are pretty much opposites. This means that we might find it hard to get along, but we could be a very effective combination if we learned to work together. We cancel out each others' weaknesses: I see the big picture, my colleague can fill in the detail. I am a risk junkie, and my colleague might just save me from myself. Equally, I will probably find opportunities which my colleague would avoid. I am good with people and building alliances, my colleague is very good with facts. We could make a very good team together, if we knew how to work together. The danger is that we will spend our whole time talking about different things and irritating each other. I will get frustrated by my colleague nagging me for detail and bringing up problems and risks. My colleague will be frustrated that I am all impractical ideas and no recognition of the need to deal with detail, risks and facts. We can not even agree on the time of day when we should meet.

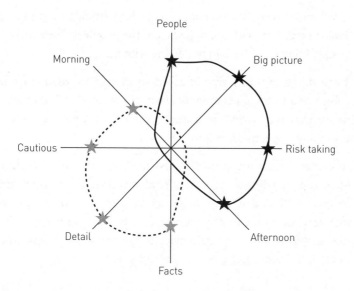

Figure 7.3 Style compass for me and my colleague

The style compass quickly tells me what I need to do. First, I need to recognise that my colleague may be different, but could be a very valuable ally. I should treasure and cherish this relationship. That means I need to make an effort to adapt, understand and influence my colleague. To adapt to my colleague I will have to make some adjustments to how I normally work:

- I will make a heroic effort, wake up early and arrange a morning meeting.

- I will make an effort to understand as much detail and as many of the risks of my idea as possible. And I will not roll my eyes in frustration when I am asked for endless amounts of further detail which I probably do not have. I will be prepared for a longer meeting than I like.

- I will ask for help and advice in dealing with the detail and risks and mustering all the facts to make the case: I will recognise him as the expert in these areas and quietly flatter him by deferring to his expertise. I will treat him as an equal partner who plays a vital role in making this all happen.

- I will make my colleague happy by dealing with all the stuff he hates: I will deal with the politics and the people. Where there is risk, I will take the lead in dealing with it.

If I can do all of this, I should avoid an immediate road crash in the form of a massive personality clash. If I do this well, then over time we may well strike up a very productive partnership which plays to our respective strengths.

You can complete the style compass in your head. It is a simple tool to use in advance of any critical meeting. Do it well, and colleagues will find it easy to get along with you: they will not understand or care why they find it easy to work with you. That is the magic of effective influence: it is unseen and apparently unforced. Influence helps people to help you.

Summary

We all live at the centre of our own worlds. This leads us to make a very natural and very dangerous mistake. We think that persuading and influencing is about getting our ideas out of our heads and into other people's heads. This leads to a war of the worlds: my world against your world. There is no good outcome to this war. No one surrenders their own world.

Influencers do what Copernicus did five hundred years ago. Copernicus rediscovered that the earth is not at the centre of the universe, much to the horror of the Church. Influencers discover that they are not at the centre of the universe. They need to see the world from a different perspective: they need to see the world from the perspective of the people they want to influence. This is the art of walking in other people's shoes.

When we see the world through the eyes of others we do not need to agree with their view, or like their view. We only need to understand it. Their view of the world can normally be summed up in a short script about who they are and what they are. It is a self-image which they normally advertise fairly clearly: you do not need to be a genius to work out what people think of themselves. If in doubt, spend some time around the water cooler and listen to the gossip. Gossip is good. In between the nonsense and trivia, there will be nuggets of gold as the characters and actions of colleagues are dissected by the gossips.

Once we understand someone's script and style, we can start to play the right tune the right way. Only when we see our agenda through other people's eyes can we understand what is attractive about it, and what its fatal flaws may be. If we play the right tune, then we will find that we can become the Pied Piper of our firm: everyone will follow us willingly.

Chapter 8

The spider's web: building incremental commitment

There is a huge difference between persuasion and influence. Persuasion encourages someone to do something once. Influence is about encouraging them to keep on doing something and to keep on supporting you. It lasts and is based on voluntary commitment. Influence is the gift that keeps on giving.

There are ways of persuading people to do something once. Charity muggers ('chuggers') can relieve you of a few dollars in the street; door-to-door salesmen persuade you to buy stuff you do not need; store salesmen can make you spend more than you intended. There are plenty of tactics for achieving such one-off success. It is hard work. It can be even harder work to persuade the same person a second time: this time they will be more cautious. In contrast, if you have influenced someone well, they will keep on returning to you time and again. Persuasion is a quick fix; influence is the lasting solution.

At the heart of the commitment process is reciprocity. Building commitment is tit for tat: you should give and take at every stage. The most common mistakes in building commitment come from ignoring this simple principle. The top three errors are:

- **Expecting too much, too soon**. Don't ask to marry someone within five minutes of meeting them: you are unlikely to get lucky. The commitment process is incremental. You have to build trust slowly on both sides. Start with the small requests ('would you like dinner?') before you get to the big requests.

- **Giving but not taking**. The urge to impress can be fatal. We want to make a good impression, so we keep on giving. And then we get taken for granted: we become a slave, not a partner. It is very hard to change that relationship once the expectations have been set.

- **Taking but not giving**. We meet the important person, ask for their help and get it. Delighted, we ask for another favour later. And another, and another. And then suddenly we find we can no longer meet the important person: their diary and door is closed to us. We are not a partner to them: we are a pain in the backside.

Be patient. Take your time. Give and take. Become the trusted partner. This is a different mindset from the crude world of persuasion, which is all about doing a deal now and moving on to the next sucker fast. Influencers are playing for bigger stakes with longer lasting rewards.

Building lasting influence requires commitment, from both sides. You are building a partnership. Here we explore how to build commitment from a cold start. The challenge is to become the trusted partner of a stranger: they do not know you, but you want their support. There are six elements to the commitment process:

1 The hook.
2 Making commitment a two-way street.
3 Using territory well.
4 Building a tribe: belonging, meaning and recognition.
5 Gaining commitment by giving control.
6 Public commitment, private challenge.

In practice, most of us spend most of our time building influence with people we already know. If you are in this happy position, you can skip the section on 'the hook' which is all about finding your way into webs of influence from which you are currently excluded.

1 The hook

Most journeys fail not because of storms along the way, but because we never find the time, opportunity or courage to start out in the first place. The hardest step is the first step. And this is true of influencing. How do we influence someone we have never met? Why will they choose to meet us? And behind this simple question lurks the ever present fear of rejection: rejection by the switchboard, rejection by the personal assistant and rejection by the person we want to influence.

This first step is hard because:

- We may not know what the right sort of hook is for our target.
- Our target may be hard to access, behind protective secretaries.
- Few of us actually enjoy cold calling: we need courage and a few techniques to help us.

In practice, here are three established hooks you can reliably use:

1 Personal introductions.
2 The teaser.
3 Ask for advice.

To see how the hook works, we will look at a real example. I wanted to start a bank. That requires at least $1 billion of capital. I checked my personal bank account. I was at least $999 million short of the required capital. So I needed to find an existing bank which would act as a partner and put up $1 billion or more. That meant I needed to talk to the CEOs of some banks. Not only did I not have a billion dollars in spare change, my contacts book was completely devoid of bank CEOs. I needed a hook to get them interested.

Personal introductions

The first step was to find some personal introductions. This is where the Kevin Bacon game is helpful. Kevin Bacon is a film star. The game proposes that no one is more than six degrees of separation away from him: the challenge is to prove it. This game was put to the test by the BBC in 2009. They gave 40 parcels to people around the world. The goal was to get the parcel to a scientist in Boston, Marc Vidal, by passing the parcel on to someone they already knew on first name terms who they thought might be closer to the scientist. From the depths of rural Kenya and elsewhere, it took on average six steps to reach Vidal. However, of the 40 packages that the BBC started with, only three made it to the final destination. That sums up the nature of targeted networking. We may only be six steps away from the person we want to meet, but knowing which six steps to take is very hard. We can expect to set out in the wrong direction more than nine times out of ten. The journey may be short, but it is not easy. Persistence is required.

The Vidal experiment was not a freak result. Microsoft examined 30 billion messages on its instant messaging service, used by 180 million people, and found that the average separation between people was 6.6 steps. The good news is that we live in a small world: if we work at it, we can find a way through to anyone we need to find.

In practice, this meant I talked to anyone and everyone about the new bank idea. If they liked the idea it was natural to then ask if they knew anyone who might be interested. I did not restrict the request to CEOs: I was happy to meet other senior bankers who could either be part of the team, or could validate the plan, or could take me one step closer to the right CEO. If they did not like the idea, then I could still ask them if they knew anyone who might advise on the idea. By conceding on the big request (support for the new bank) they would return the compliment by conceding on the small request (giving the names of some more people to talk to). Eventually I found my way to several CEOs.

The teaser

Even with a personal introduction, it made sense to strengthen the hook with a problem solution offer. The problem solution offer is the staple of much advertising: use our product to remove stains better; our product relieves headaches faster; our computers are more lightweight and powerful. We may dislike such advertising, but it works. We have a problem (dirty clothes, headache etc) and the advertising offers a solution. To be really effective, the pitch should be personal. So the next step was a short letter which looked like this:

> Dear Mr xxxx
>
> I am writing on the advice of John Jones[1] who thought it might be of mutual benefit for us to explore a new business proposal. We are[2] developing a corporate middle market bank[3] which can fill a gap in your portfolio between your successful SME and corporate banking businesses[4]. We expect the bank to achieve $50 million pre tax profits within five years.[5]
>
> I represent a group of senior bankers who have been developing this proposal and can form the start up team to bring this idea to market fast.[6]
>
> In the first instance, it will make sense for us to have an exploratory discussion[7] to see if this idea fits with your current portfolio and priorities. I will call your secretary[8] next week to arrange a suitable time to meet you.[9]
>
> Yours truly,

No hook letter is perfect, and it does not need to be. It simply needs to work. The letter above worked as a hook. Note that it was a letter, not an email. Emails are deleted faster than letters hit the waste basket: the letter shows you have made an effort and there is a chance that it will be read and remembered. The principles behind the letter also apply to a phone pitch or any other initial contact where you need to hook someone into an initial meeting. The main principles behind the hook in the letter are numbered and explained below:

1 This is the personal introduction, right up front to grab attention. The CEO knew and respected John Jones (an alias). The goal was to stop the secretary putting the letter in the waste basket immediately. Whether writing or speaking, you need to get past the first sentence. A weak first sentence leads to switch off.

2 Note the positive verb. Not 'might' or 'hoping to' or 'thinking about'. We are doing it, the only question is who with: if you refuse, your arch-rivals may decide to be the partner instead. In truth, we were still at the hope and wish stage. Project confidence, not uncertainty.

3 Be very clear about what the idea is, so they see it is specific and they understand it.

4 Make it highly personalised to this bank; be positive about their existing portfolio, otherwise you will encourage a defensive reaction and denial.

5 Size the prize: it is worth the CEO getting out of bed for this. It is not something for a junior analyst to look into. It answers the question: why should I bother?

6 Be credible: show there is support, momentum and commitment. In truth, the senior bankers were interested but were not going to give up their day jobs until a deal was done. This answers the question: do I believe what is being said? In other sorts of pitches endorsements from bosses, clients, experts, sports stars can all work.

7 This is an easy ask: invest an hour of your time to see if you want $50 million a year. This is the first step of incremental commitment.

8 The CEO will not read this letter, the secretary will. Promise to follow up. When you follow up she will have forgotten about

or ignored your letter, so be ready to resend it. Second time round she will take it seriously because she now knows you will follow up, so she will show the letter to the CEO and ask for advice. The hardest task can be getting past the switchboard to the secretary.

9 Keep it short. The more you write, the more there is for them to disagree with or dislike.

We can't always dangle a $50 million hook in front of someone. But there are plenty of other teasers which are routinely used to hook new customers. We have all been hooked by these at one time or another.

- Research firms offer a summary of findings for free; the full report comes at full price.

- You can read part of a book on Amazon for free, and then decide if you want to commit to paying for the whole book.

- Free product samples or test drives of cars are simple and honest ways of letting people make their minds up before making a larger commitment.

- Consulting firms offer an initial diagnostic phase at low or no cost: they always find problems which, fortunately, they can solve. At a price.

Ask for advice

There is an even easier, and often better, way of hooking people. Instead of offering them something, ask for something. The one thing people are normally happy to give is advice. By giving advice it shows that our judgement is valued and that we have some expertise and knowledge about the subject in question. By asking for advice, we flatter someone.

Ask for advice

Asking for advice is as simple as it sounds. I wanted to gain some clients in France, so I wrote to various targets saying I was doing research on Anglo-French leadership: the theory was that France has a different and potentially better leadership model than the UK. Could I come and discuss this with them? As a teaser which reinforced my credentials, I sent an article with the summary of my findings on Anglo-Saxon leadership. The more senior the French business people were, the happier they were to meet me and tell me exactly why French leadership was superior to anything the nefarious Brits could imagine. Ask for advice, flatter and the hook has done its job.

Within a firm, most senior managers are delighted to give people the benefit of their wisdom. It costs them little and reinforces their self-image as respected, important and knowledgeable people. Asking for advice gently exploits the vanity of managers, and leads to a more productive conversation than daring to offer advice. The curse of smart people is that they like to show they are smart. Really smart people have the self-confidence to avoid this trap and to appear humble.

> asking for advice gently exploits the vanity of managers

If you ask for advice, ask early. Asking for advice is not just about flattering egos. It also works because you give your colleague a sense of control and influence over the outcome. If they control the outcome, they own it. People rarely oppose something which they feel they own and control. The later you leave the request for advice, the less influence your colleague has over the outcome and the less commitment they will feel towards it.

For instance, I was asked to do a valuation for a bank. I did it and thought I did good work. It was shot down in flames by the bank's financial department. Bank accounts are arcane: the credit crunch suggests that not many bank executives understood their own bank's accounts very well. The high priests of bank finance could shoot down an outsider's analysis of their position with ease. Even if I was right, they could prove that I was wrong. There is a general principle which is never argue with babies, taxi drivers or god: even if you are right it will do you no good. To that list you can add actuaries, financial experts and other technical experts of all sorts: never argue with them on their favourite technical subject.

Despite that bruising experience, I was asked to repeat the exercise for another bank. This time I made no mistake. Immediately I set up a meeting with the finance department which would review and vet the final valuation. They waxed lyrical about tier 1 and tier 2 capital ratios and Basel III. I did my best to look interested. I then checked in with them regularly during the assignment to get more advice. By the time we produced the final valuation, they felt it was their valuation. They endorsed it strongly and the board accepted it without question.

Ask for advice early, and keep on asking for it. Share ownership of the final result with anyone who can either derail or endorse the outcome.

2 Making commitment a two-way street

Commitment is a two-way street, but is often treated as a one-way street. The goal of the commitment process is to achieve trusted partner status. As trusted partners you will work together as equals towards a common goal. If you are to be equals and you are both to work together, you have to establish that mindset from the outset. This is commonly missed. Some people demand commitment and others give commitment without reciprocating. One way commitments are not healthy and fail to achieve influence.

All of this is obvious, but as George Orwell wrote, 'Seeing what is in front of your nose requires constant struggle.' The goal is obvious, but many people are unaware of it. And achieving the goal is far harder than stating it. In many cases, commitment ends up as a one-way street.

Most firms have a few sociopaths (often including the CEO) who believe commitment is all one-way: they demand complete loyalty and passion and simply do not understand that loyalty has to be reciprocated. For them, being a team player means 'you accept my orders or you are not on my team'. Give and take means giving orders and blame, while taking all the credit. These are rarely pleasant relationships, except for the sociopath who will be very happy with the way the world revolves around himself.

The more common one-way street is where we ourselves are making all the commitment. This is where we play into the hands of the sociopaths and the merely idle. In our desire to impress and show how good we are, we work harder and harder to show what we can do. We land up in a very dysfunctional relationship. Each time we impress, we simply raise expectations. That forces us to work harder than ever, and we get nothing in return. We have not created a partnership of influence, we have turned ourselves into willing slaves. Influence is based on a partnership of mutual commitment and obligation.

To create mutual commitment we have to ask for commitment from the other side: this can feel very unnatural. Most people dislike imposing on others unless there is a clear need. Well, there is a clear need: unless both sides make an effort for each other there can be no partnership of trust. This is as true of marriage partnerships as it is of business partnerships.

The process of mutual commitment has to start from the first meeting: the nature of the relationship needs to be established immediately. The longer you leave it, the harder it is to change the nature of the relationship. In practice, this means you have to ask for something even from the first meeting. It may only be a token effort, but it sets the tone and the expectations going forwards: this is a partnership, not a slave relationship. Here are some simple things I have asked clients to do for me after first meetings:

- Forward a link to an article which the client mentioned.
- Clarify a small piece of data which we discussed.
- Check, and report, on the views of two colleagues.

These are small tasks which are a big first step. Your partner has made the vital transition from being passive to being active. As a passive counterparty they do little more than act as judge and jury: they may be entertained or even impressed by how well you perform. But they are not helping you perform. They are spectators, not partners and you will have little influence over them. By making them into active partners, even in a small way, you have set the relationship onto a far more productive path.

As soon as your client or colleague has done some homework for you, they have established a platform for building two-way commitment. You are now in a position to praise and thank them for their work. Giving praise is a power position: it is a positive way of passing judgement. By giving praise you have evened up what may have started as an unequal relationship. You have also created the excuse for reciprocating with a favour of your own and for

> giving praise is a power position: it is a positive way of passing judgement

exploring more ideas. The process of tit for tat has started: the expectation has been set that you will both help each other. The one-way street is becoming a two-way street, but you need to push this new psychological contract further.

At an early stage, set up a meeting away from the client's home territory. 'Early' means the second meeting. When the client (or colleague) is in their office they are on their territory. You are the visitor that they have allowed in, and they are the gracious (or not so gracious) host. The guest–visitor relationship is not a partnership. You need to break that mindset fast. Find an excuse to meet on your territory or on neutral territory: in the canteen or at a restaurant. Once they have moved out of their territory, the nature of the relationship changes: you are now more like equals working together. The conversation can change from what you will do for them: it becomes what you can do together. You migrate more easily to the partnership model where you can start to have real influence.

3 Using territory well

Humans are territorial. We all mark out our spaces. Photographs, mementoes and certificates all proclaim that this office or cubicle is someone's territory. And we all tend to feel more comfortable in our home territory than in the alien world of a board room, or the office of a customer or senior executive.

And different scripts go with different territories. The most basic script is the ask-give script. Typically, when you go to someone else's territory you are asking them for something. When they come to you, they are asking you for something. The asker has to do all the hard work, while the giver sits as judge and jury deciding whether to give, and if so on what terms. This is not a healthy influencing script: influence is about creating a partnership of equals which does not come from an ask-give script.

The second sort of territorial script is the inspection script. For instance, the bank may consider giving you a loan (after you have visited their territory) and will then inspect your business to see if they believe all the wonderful things you claimed about your business. And bosses are always inspecting teams. Again, these are not healthy scripts for a partnership.

The easiest way to get to a partnership script is to find neutral territory. On neutral territory, the inspection script and the ask-give scripts quickly disappear.

So how do you get onto neutral territory fast? Ask someone out. It may be as simple as getting breakfast together before work, or agreeing to have lunch in the canteen together. Or it can be as elaborate as corporate entertaining. On neutral territory the conversation changes. You have the chance to talk socially, to discover mutual interests and build rapport. Any business discussion more naturally becomes a partnership discussion rather than an ask-give discussion. You build relationships better over pasta than over PowerPoint.

> you build relationships better over pasta than over PowerPoint

The territory principle helps corporate entertaining work. The vendor is no longer on the buyer's territory. The buyer recognises that the rules of the game have changed and an entirely different set of conversations happen at the sporting or cultural event. There is a surfeit of corporate entertaining opportunities out there, and the person you want to entertain may well be sick of corporate entertaining. So make sure you find an opportunity which reflects their personal interests. Or find something which will give them bragging rights back at the office: unusual places, events or speakers are a good start.

4 Building a tribe: belonging, meaning and recognition

In many firms loyalty is a one-way street: the firm demands loyalty, passion and commitment right up to the moment where you are right-sized, downsized, off-shored, best-shored, re-engineered, outsourced or just plain fired. Unrequited love and unrequited loyalty rarely last long. To sustain commitment managers need to give as well as take. There are two basic needs any firm or manager must fulfil to generate voluntary commitment:

1 Belonging and meaning: I belong to a community worth belonging to.

2 Recognition: I am recognised and valued by others for what I do.

Belonging and meaning

The tribal instinct runs deep. We all have a need to belong to a group. The desire to belong is universal. The way we

> the desire to belong is universal

dress proclaims our tribe: the armed forces take great care to show which military tribe everyone belongs to with a range of carefully differentiated uniforms. The corporate tribe has subtle dress codes which vary by type of business, function, level and occasion. Even rebellious teenagers invest a huge amount of time and money acquiring an identity which allows them to belong to one of the ever shifting tribes of teenage fashion and music. Fortunately, most managers do not have to go to war or become a teenager again to understand and use the power of belonging and meaning.

The power of belonging sustains loyalty in even the most adverse conditions. Sports fans are a good example. For instance, the New Orleans Saints were so unsuccessful in the 1980s they became known as the 'Ain'ts'. Their fans were mortified and some took to wearing paper bags over their heads. They kept on supporting, but it was painful. Sports fans identify with their team: winning teams make their fans feel like winners. Losing teams make their fans feel like wearing paper bags over their heads to maintain their anonymity.

To this day, there are organisations which build extraordinary esprit de corps and gain extraordinary commitment from staff. Many of these are elites: staff at McKinsey or Goldman Sachs feel they are part of an elite and put in huge effort to maintain that status. But you do not have to pay staff vast salaries to create an esprit de corps and a sense of belonging to something special. Soldiers in most British regiments are poorly paid but hugely proud of their regiment and the hundreds of years of tradition they represent. More mundanely, Teach First is an example of how a sense of belonging to something special builds esprit de corps and extraordinary voluntary commitment.

Teach First has perhaps the world's least attractive recruiting proposition for university undergraduates: do not go and get a huge salary at a bank or consulting company. Join us and have two years of grief teaching in the most challenging secondary schools in the UK. The concept was so unattractive that we could find no graduates from the top universities teaching in the schools we wanted to serve. So we had to change perceptions. Now look at the proposition through the new lens. If you join Teach First you will:

- join an elite
- be trained to be a leader of the future, in education, business or beyond
- be doing something well worthwhile
- work with other exceptional people like yourself
- do something with high social value and respect: it is supported by prime ministers and royalty alike
- gain experience which all top employers value greatly: most top recruiters sponsor and support Teach First.

Viewed through this lens, Teach First is highly attractive. Nearly 10% of Oxford and Cambridge final year undergraduates apply to get onto the programme each year. The messages which Teach First uses are the same that any manager can use to create a sense of belonging:

- We are doing something special and worthwhile.
- We are an elite that is capable of achieving this great mission.

In most firms there are teams which clearly look, feel and act as if they are special: they have fierce loyalty to each other and work hard to achieve their goals. It might be a skunkworks developing a new product, or the creative team that develops brilliant advertising, or the IT group which does great things with technology. The two tricks to building this special sense of belonging are:

1 Show that the team is doing something special and worthwhile.
2 Tell the team that they are a special group.

Once people have this sense of belonging, their commitment is voluntary and they become self policing. They perform not because the boss tells them to. They perform because they do not want to let their colleagues down, and they do not want to let themselves down. Peer group pressure is far more intense than boss pressure. Boss pressure is about compliance; peer group pressure is about commitment.

When people have a sense of belonging and meaning, even mundane work becomes meaningful. There is a well rehearsed story of a king going to a building site in the medieval era. He asked the first worker, who looked sullen and unhappy, what he was doing. 'I am getting cold shifting lumps of earth around,' came the reply. The king asked a second person the same question. 'Building a building, can't you see?' came the second reply. The king asked a third worker the same question. This worker seemed full of energy and enthusiasm and was working twice as hard as the others. The worker replied with enthusiasm: 'I am serving God and building a temple to Him so that future generations can worship him. This is my monument.' Shifting lumps of earth has little meaning; building a cathedral has great meaning. The same work can either be made meaningless or meaningful. Make work meaningful and commitment rises.

Recognition is a tool which is at the disposal of all influencers. As we look back at the people who have influenced us positively, they are likely to be teachers, parents or even colleagues and bosses who recognised our talents and forgave our very minor defects. We respond well to recognition. Very few people think that they are over-recognised for their talents and contribution: most of us think we are greatly under-recognised and undervalued. That is a wonderful opportunity for an influencer. It allows an influencer to fill a void in someone's life and to stand out from other people who do not give enough recognition.

> most of us think we are greatly under-recognised and undervalued

Recognition is an art form: it can be done poorly or well. Done poorly, it is insincere and sounds insincere. One minute managers who throw around condescending and generic compliments quickly lose credibility. Good praise is specific, personal and detailed. For instance, if someone helps you:

- Explain why the action was useful to you.
- Explain what was useful about it: what it achieved.

Private recognition is a start; public recognition is even better. It works because it:

- focuses debate on agreements, not disagreements
- creates an emotional debt to you from the people being praised
- forms the impression of a bandwagon which is starting to roll
- builds support for you: people do not change a public position they have taken
- reinforces the behaviour you want to focus on.

Recognition is not just about recognising people who agree with you. It can also be used to turn disagreement into agreement. The best way to win an argument, like winning a war, is without fighting. I learned the art of using recognition to turn adversity into advantage when I worked at P&G. We called it the art of the nice save, and was mainly used in trying to tame our creative but occasionally wayward advertising agencies.

We would be presented with wild, creative, brilliant and utterly useless advertising ideas by one of our agencies. If we criticised it, the fragile but supersized egos of the creative team would throw a tantrum. So instead we used the nice save. We would identify the one or two positive things about the idea (like they bothered to mention our brand in between the shots of line dancing hippos in sunglasses). We would get them to work up the good aspects. This would make them more open to sidelining and eventually dropping the hippos. Always look for the positives, give praise and recognition: people become less defensive and more open to change once they feel their extraordinary talents and effort have been properly recognised.

Recognition need not be devious. It can also be simple and direct. John Timpson owns a chain of 400 shoe repair shops which carry his name. Cobbling is not glamorous work. Many of the shops are little more than dark holes with staff who work on modest wages. The key to it is not great cobbling. The key is great customer service. The problem is that cobblers relate to soles more than to souls: they deal with shoes better than they deal with people. Timpson could not regulate great customer service at 400 remote locations. He had to build commitment to it from all the staff. For Timpson, the commitment comes from very public recognition of the right behaviours. He drives around the country with a trunk full of rewards and his goal is to give praise ten times as much as he criticises: criticism delivers control, praise delivers commitment. He needs commitment because a control and compliance culture does not deliver great customer service. The power of recognition, reinforced with annual awards, newsletters and other public forms of recognition, drive voluntary commitment and the desired service levels.

5 Gaining commitment by giving control

Management control is seen to be good: managers who are not in control are not doing a good job. From this simple starting point, a whole host of evils emerge. Many managers think that control means reporting, measuring, monitoring, assessing and praising or rebuking. This is control, but it is alienating because staff prefer to be trusted than controlled. The growth of technology means that the level of reporting and control today is beyond the wildest dreams of the greatest control freak of years gone by. In the days of pen, paper and the steam train reporting had to be less frequent and less intense. Modern management speak talks empowerment but practises control: we live in an age of distrust.

> staff prefer to be trusted than controlled

There is an alternative to heavy management control: self-control and control through peer pressure. These forms of control are voluntary and lead to a commitment culture, not a compliance culture. At a basic level, most people want to stay in control of their lives and their jobs. If we are being controlled by someone else we tend to resent it.

Good influencers use the concept of self-control to induce high commitment and high performance. It is control by letting go, at least to some extent.

The power of control through self-control was very clear in a car factory where I was doing some filming for television. The factory had undergone a TQM revolution: its cars rose from near the bottom of the JD Power reliability ratings to near the top. There are many elements to TQM (total quality management) which experts will wax lyrical about. These can include: measurement, designing quality in, six sigma quality, consistency of process, eliminating errors and not waiting to inspect and fix errors at the end of the process. But on the production line, the revolution was about the people and the nature of control.

Frank had worked at the plant for 30 years. He remembered the bad old days. Supervisors supervised, inspectors inspected and workers were treated as dumb and unreliable machines that had to be monitored closely. It was a compliance culture which encouraged warfare between workers and management: no wonder product quality sucked. With TQM the locus of power shifted. Suddenly, Frank and his colleagues on the line were responsible for quality. At every work station there was a wall of graphs which showed how they were performing. The data was not the private information of supervisors and inspectors – they had been largely eliminated. This was the public data of each work group. Frank proudly showed me all the data: it was his chance to show how well the team was doing. There was rivalry with other work groups to see who could do best: no one wanted to be the team that was letting the rest of their colleagues down.

With the shift of power and control, Frank and his colleagues saw themselves differently. They were no longer the victims of callous and useless management. They had become champions of quality and production: they were in control of their own destiny. By moving from a compliance to a commitment culture the plant saved itself.

Frank's story is not an exception. In Chicago, an old detergents plant was in trouble. Production for a couple of products was being shifted to another city. Another product was being developed by the group, but if the factory wanted it, then they had to bid for it against other factories in the same group. With an old factory and old-style labour relations they looked doomed. Management and workers could not even agree on the length of work breaks, let alone changing working practices enough to win the bid. So management made a radical decision. They decided to leave the factory for six weeks and let the workers figure out if and how they should bid. Six weeks later, the workers had transformed their own working practices and put in a winning bid. They had also redefined the job of management who had to negotiate their way back into the plant. When management controlled the plant, workers had no ownership or commitment. When it was their plant and their problem, they become zealous advocates of best working practices.

The unglamorous world of making pumps in Brazil is not an obvious place to start looking for a management revolution. But Ricardo Semler, who runs Semco, has become a folk hero for managing by letting go. He claims not to have made a decision in 12 years: the workers make all the decisions: pay, conditions, hiring managers. And it all started with the canteen. As in many firms, everyone liked to whine about the canteen. This annoyed Semler so much that he told the workers they could run the canteen. The complaints stopped and the canteen improved. From that early start, Semler discovered the power of giving control away.

Voluntary commitment is not just about money as the evidence of the car plant workers, sports fans or any number of voluntary organisations demonstrate. We have to look beyond money if we want to build lasting commitment. This is just as well for most influencers, since we are not normally in a position to bribe colleagues or clients.

Giving control is like delegation. You can delegate away control, but you can not delegate away accountability. Managers should always be held to account. But you can change the nature of your role. You no longer add value by ordering, controlling, measuring and assessing. You add value by supporting and coaching, clearing political logjams, securing resources and managing other stakeholders such as top management. In other words, you create a new role where you add real value to the team, instead of simply being another layer of bureaucracy. Delegating control does not destroy management: it enhances the role of management.

> you can delegate away control, but you can not delegate away accountability

6 Public commitment, private challenge

Imagine a firm where they have a thorough induction process. First, there is the normal health and safety briefing. Then all the men are taken down to the post room. There, they have to undress. One by one they are led to a blood-stained bench where an evil looking person gets out a large knife and circumcises them in front of all the other new employees. If anyone cries out in pain, they fail. They are all left there overnight to let their wounds heel. Those who pass have their bodies painted and they then spend the next 30 days going round the office wearing nothing but their body paint. Everyone can plainly see they have passed the circumcision test. After a few more tests, those who pass get to pick a girl from the office. This is a firm which might not recruit many people, but those who joined up would be pretty deeply committed.

This firm is called the Dogon. The Dogon are a traditional society living in the barren scrub of sub-Saharan Mali. The local blacksmith does the circumcising on a blood-stained rock. The surrounding rocks are covered in murals: one shows a long snake which will eat anyone who fails the test. Other murals represent different families, and yet more retell the secrets and legends of the Dogon into which the young men will be introduced. The Dogon are not alone in having elaborate rites of passage. Other brutal rites can be found in most traditional societies, from Africa to Australia and the South Pacific. Slightly less brutal initiation rites and passing out ceremonies are common in the armed forces and even fraternities and sororities on the campus of American universities.

In tribal societies, belonging is not just nice to have: it is essential to survival. To be cast out from such a society means death. Belonging makes it worthwhile for aspiring members of the tribe to go through such unpleasant rites. Equally, the public commitment reinforces the sense of belonging. Public commitment and belonging reinforce each other.

Public commitments are powerful commitments: they offer no going back. For instance, I once made the mistake of deciding to run a marathon. I trained, and then realised it was all too much like hard work and I did not have the time. I dropped the idea. Then I made the same mistake again, with a twist. This time I told four colleagues that I would run. They laughed and told everyone else: when challenged, I confirmed I was going to run. Suddenly, I was committed. There was no going back and no excuses. Letting myself down is not great: letting everyone else down is far worse. So I trained and ran and completed the marathon. And I will never make the same mistake a third time.

The principle of public commitment runs both ways. It can be positive or negative. Once a colleague has taken a position in public, they find it very hard to unwind that position. They will go through more or less any intellectual hoops to justify what they have said or done. The need to self-justify came through clearly with a focus group of owners of outsized off-road vehicles in London. There is not much need for off-road driving in the city. When they were asked about the environmental aspects of driving such a car in the city, the mood turned ugly. Typical responses were:

- A car with a family in it is far better than all the buses which never have anyone in them.
- Old Land Rovers have the same wheelbase as a new Mini.
- We only drive 6,000 miles a year, which is far more responsible than people who drive 40,000 miles a year in a smaller car.
- At least we don't fly so much.
- Electric cars are even worse because of battery disposal and all the power station emissions for powering the batteries.
- People are just envious of us.
- It's a free society, isn't it?

There is not much logic in any of the answers, but there is plenty of self-justification. Once people have taken a position, they defend it vigorously. For the influencer, this has two implications:

1 Manage conflict in private: do not let anyone take a public stance against your interests.

2 Publicise agreements and commitments quickly and widely.

Manage conflict in private

Managing conflict in private is a basic requirement of influence. This is especially important where you have a new idea which you want to promote. If you raise your idea in a meeting, say goodbye to your idea. Meetings are designed to kill ideas and to discourage anyone else from daring to have ideas. In the words of one French *chef du cabinet* (head of a large government department): 'Meetings are a wonderful opportunity to sabotage the plans of other ministries.' The last time I made the mistake of having an idea in a meeting, I found myself at the wrong end of a shooting gallery. The bullets all came in the form of helpful questions:

'How much will it cost? Is it in your budget? Whose budget is it? Who will work on it, is anyone available? Have you done a risk assessment? Have you talked this through with HR/finance/IT/ ops/Japan/my great aunt's parrot? We've never done this before, so how is it possible? We did it before and it doesn't work, does it? Where's the business case?'

This is the normal reaction to new ideas in meetings. The easiest way to prove you are smart is to ask smart questions and identify the main risks: this has the benefit of protecting the firm against risk. It also kills the idea and removes the need to take any further action. Conversely, encouraging ideas is dangerous and may lead to more work.

Unless you know you have support, keep critical discussions in private. The dividing line between a private and public meeting is two people. As soon as there is a third person the meeting is essentially public and each person is taking a position: the discussion becomes a negotiation. In private, people can be more open, more honest and more flexible. If they disagree with you, you can still go back to them another time to address their concerns and find a way forward. Once they have raised doubts in public, they will keep on reinforcing their position. The need for self-justification will overwhelm the need for logic.

There are some basic principles for managing these private disagreements:

- Listen.
- Find agreements not disagreements.
- Focus on interests, not positions.
- Size the prize.
- Focus on facts not opinions.

These principles are covered in detail in the following chapters. The common theme behind these principles is that good influencers do not just win an argument: they win an ally. The goal is not to beat your opponent into submission with the brilliance of your analysis. The goal is to find a win–win outcome which both sides like.

Publicise agreements

When you have agreement, make it public. This is where meetings are useful. Meetings should never be used to make a decision: give people a choice and they may make the wrong decision. Meetings should only be used to confirm in public the decisions which have been reached in private. This public confirmation of private deals is vital: it gives reassurance to each individual that they are not alone in giving support to your idea. No one wants to be the first to jump. But with the right choreography, you can persuade everyone to jump at the same time. The meeting is where they jump.

> meetings should never be used to make a decision

The 'right choreography' is about building confidence and consensus. The Japanese describe this process as *nemawashi*. It takes time but is highly effective. Working for a Japanese bank in Tokyo and an American bank in New York showed me the power of the process. In Japan, months passed before we finally came to a decision. When we got to the formal decision making meeting, the decision had already been made. We were simply confirming all the consensus which had been reached in private. Implementing the decision was rapid, smooth and effective.

In New York, we had to meet an urgent deadline and presented our recommendations as soon as we had done the analysis, but without any *nemawashi*. A riot erupted in the meeting. The decision was pushed through anyway. For months afterwards, the decision was being sabotaged, rival plans were being promoted, power barons were doing their own things. It was a coruscating whirl of activity and initiative. Huge talent and effort was expended in going precisely nowhere. Ultimately, the Japanese tortoise was much faster than the American hare.

The process of building confidence is a search for agreement. The agreement process is incremental. You are managing a series of persuasive conversations in parallel. At each stage of the conversation, you are trying to find areas of agreement which allow you to build consensus and confidence.

For instance, one large telecoms company told us that they had a very high-performance culture: it was the secret of their success. We suspected that they had a low-performance culture which was supported by the legacy of a legal monopoly over fixed line telecoms. The legacy was wearing out and they needed to change the culture. There was little point in arguing about their opinion. So we gathered the following facts:

- Employees were 27 times more likely to die in service than to be fired for poor performance; this was not because all their employees were getting killed, but because no one was getting fired.

- 92% of staff were rated as average or above, which is mathematically impossible.

- IBM fires the weakest 10% of its managers every year.

We refused any discussion about the performance culture. All we did for the first few weeks was to validate the findings. We asked the managers to confirm that the facts were correct. When they gave us confirmation, we published the facts and the confirmation. As the deluge of data became overwhelming the claims about being a high-performance organisation simply disappeared. We focused on areas of agreement (facts, not opinions) and publicised the partial agreements: incrementally, we were building commitment and momentum.

Summary

Away from the dramatic speeches by CEOs and gurus about excellence, passion and commitment, the daily life of managers is a hard grind. It can be like swimming through treacle. Dealing with politics, opposition and conflict; making alliances, trying to make a difference while trying to keep day-to-day operations in order.

The commitment process gives a clue as to why management is such hard work. The commitment process takes time and effort. At any one moment a manager can have a dozen commitment conversations on the go with different colleagues: each conversation will happen intermittently over days and weeks. Keeping track of each conversation and orchestrating them so that they all reach the right conclusion at the right time is a fine art and an exhausting sport.

The commitment process may be hard work, but it is worthwhile investment. Once you have created mutual commitment, you have a platform for success. You will have allies on whom you can rely. In the short term it is possible to persuade and bully people into agreement. Influencers have more ambition than persuaders. Influencers want willing and lasting commitment, whereas persuaders will settle for temporary compliance and acceptance. The commitment process separates out influencers from persuaders.

Chapter 9

Build your platform

nfluential people do not have to rely on office and status for power. They create their own form of informal power. They all have a platform which they cultivate carefully. These platforms represent a short cut to power and influence. Instead of waiting and hoping for promotion, these platforms offer influence and power in a hurry.

There are four main types of platform you can use:

1 Influential people: borrow credibility and influence.
2 Influential places: go where the power is.
3 Claims to fame: build your personal platform.
4 Agenda control: have a plan.

It is possible to grow all four sorts of influence at the same time. Influential people and places are about borrowing a platform for influence. They are short cuts to influence. At some point managers also need to acquire influence in their own right. Agenda control and having a claim to fame give managers a personal platform of influence.

1 Influential people: borrow credibility and influence

We can borrow money for the short term, perhaps on our credit cards, and we can borrow money for the long term, perhaps on our mortgage. In the same way, managers can borrow influence in both the short term and the long term. In the short term, borrowed influence comes from the power of endorsements. Long-term borrowing of power comes from patronage: making alliances with the right power barons. Both sorts of borrowing increase the influence which a manager can exert in an organisation.

Short-term borrowing: the power of endorsement

The power of endorsement became clear when I found myself at Lloyds, the reinsurance underwriting business. I had imagined it would be a highly sophisticated and complicated business underwriting the risk of oil rigs, supertankers, aircraft and football stars' feet. I was wrong. The broker went round various old fashioned desks where underwriters sat. The broker pulled out a piece of paper with a $3 billion risk on a North Sea oil rig. The underwriter looked at the piece of paper. 'OK,' he said after about ten seconds, 'If it's good enough for Charlie, Tom and Jamie it's good enough for me. I'll take a $50 million line.' He had just committed his firm to $50 million of risk on the basis that people he trusted had also taken up some of the risk. Some time later Lloyds was submerged in bad risks and nearly went bust: assessing risk on the basis of which of your friends have signed up was perhaps not smart enough.

Effective managers learn to put the power of endorsement to their advantage. Business plans, promotions and new ideas are not judged just on the basis of the idea. They are also judged on the quality of the people behind the idea. In the same way, venture capitalists do not judge a new business idea just on the basis of a business plan. They back the manager as much as they back the plan. There is good reason for this. A good team will improve an average plan and will make molehills out of mountains. The 'B' team will struggle to live up to its promises. Until you have an established track record, you will be regarded as the 'B' team: you will be judged on performance, not on potential.

Long-term borrowing of power: the power of patronage

When Kensington Palace was first built it gave great amusement to the peasants of Kensington. They would gather outside and watch the high and mighty lords and ladies arriving in their extravagant court dress. It was like watching film stars arriving for a premier, but without the respect and adulation which film stars receive. For their part, the lords and ladies would carry nosegays of perfumed herbs to protect their very refined noses from the smells of the great unwashed: in practice, however, even the lords and ladies stank. They would change their outer clothes several times a day, and they would change their underclothes three or four times a year. Everyone wanted to petition the king, but access was limited. Some people would wait for days in one of the many waiting rooms and ante chambers. The smarter petitioners would seek the patronage of aristocrats who already had access to the king. Power and money flowed from the king: the closer you were, the more influence, power and prestige you had.

Nothing has changed in government: the Prime Minister takes on the role of the king and dispenses patronage. The PM's court consists of secretaries of state, ministers, special advisers and various favoured think tanks and influencers. The closer you get to these sources of power, the more influence you wield.

The kings of the corporate world are CEOs. Hopefully, they change their underwear more often than the kings of the past. But still power and patronage flow from the CEO, and still the power barons gather round their corporate king, jostling for position and for favours. Those who do well can, like Cardinal Richelieu under Louis XIII, find fame and fortune. Those who displease the king suffer corporate execution: they are fired.

> the kings of the corporate world are CEOs

The principles of patronage apply as much in the corporate world as they did in the era of powerful kings and queens.

Access to the top is desirable, but for many managers access to a power baron is a very useful substitute. Picking the right power baron is not easy. The right power baron has two qualities:

- *Success:* they will have or acquire significant patronage in terms of bonuses, pay, promotions, projects and assignments.
- *Loyalty:* they will stick with and reward the team that helped them succeed.

Patronage is a two-way street: the patron always wants something in return for what they give. The stronger the give and take, the deeper the loyalty and commitment is likely to be. Michael demonstrated how to be a power baron when he started a new service line offering post merger integration support to clients. First, he was successful: he built the business rapidly. That gave him a pot of bonus money and influence over promotions which made him a highly attractive power baron. Second, he was fiercely loyal to his team and demanded 100% loyalty in return. His team became like a firm within a firm. Outsiders were not welcome and it became very hard to judge who was doing what inside the team. Only Michael really knew what was going on. He used success and knowledge to his advantage. At promotion time he backed his three candidates vigorously. Michael essentially bullied the promotion commission into accepting his picks: the only performance benchmark the commission had came from Michael who was clearly successful. Success and loyalty breeds dedicated followers. They also attract some of the best and most ambitious talent into his team.

Michael expects his pound of flesh in return. Total loyalty and total commitment is required. His team is like a cult: it has its own values, beliefs and ways of doing things. They are not just loyal to Michael: they are loyal to each other.

If surrendering your ego, life and career to that of an emerging power baron is a step too far, there are other weaker but still effective forms of patronage which managers can cultivate. A good mentoring relationship can be highly productive for both sides: as with all forms of patronage it should be a win–win relationship. This is what each side should expect:

- **Mentee**: gains access to a senior executive. Personal advice and support helps; an insight into how senior managers think is invaluable preparation for dealing with other senior managers; the mentor should also alert the mentee to emerging career opportunities and risks, and should be able to help break the occasional political logjam. The mentor may not give much time, but the value of each intervention can be huge.

- **Mentor**: the mentor values having eyes and ears across the organisation. Top executives distrust formal papers which are submitted to them: such papers give a warped version of the truth. They value word of mouth about what is really going on across the organisation. They also need some 'go-to' people when they need discretionary help and support on building a new idea, making a speech or preparing a meeting. Finally, most mentors are quietly flattered that emerging talent is seeking them out and values their views.

The main block to forming such relationships is normally in the mentee's head. We look at the big bosses and think of them as big bosses. We let the hierarchy get in the way of the relationship. The trick is to remember that even the biggest boss is still a human being, despite appearances to the contrary. If we treat them as humans and partners, not just as bosses, we are more likely to establish a productive relationship with them.

> even the biggest boss is still a human being

2 Influential places: go where the power is

Willie Sutton, the famous American bank robber, was asked why he robbed banks. 'Because that is where the money is,' he replied. If you want money, go where the money is. If you want fame, go where the fame is. If you want power, go where the power is.

Some people are attracted to power like moths to a light. Inevitably, some get burned in the process. The brightest source of power and influence is the organisation you represent. A few people become influential in their own right: pop stars, actors, artists and sports people can all achieve influence on their own. Some, like Bono, have presidents and prime ministers jostling to get their photo taken with them. Unless we are confident of becoming a global megastar in our own right, we need a short cut to achieving position and influence. As soon as we represent an organisation, we inherit the influence and credibility of that organisation. If we join the right part of that organisation, we multiply our influence even further.

Choice of employer

When business people meet in Japan, the first thing they do is to exchange *meishi*, business cards. To the western eye, *meishi* states someone's name, employer and position. In practice, *meishi* are guides to who should have bowed first, longest and deepest upon introduction. The person's title and company will indicate their status: Toyota is clearly more prestigious than one of its suppliers or the local corner shop. As the *meishi* are read and exchanged, vigorous bowing ensues to establish the right social order. Bowing may seem difficult to westerners, but try explaining how to shake hands to a Japanese businessman (when, how do you know it is time, how do you show you want to shake hands, how hard, how long?).

The tale of the *meishi* shows how far we depend on our employer for our status and influence. If you work for McKinsey, executives are likely to answer the phone when you call. If you are calling from Fred's Consulting Emporium, you will find it much harder to contact the CEO you wished to talk to. Every time we call, every time we state our employer's name we borrow all their credibility: we inherit the influence and power built up over years by the firm. To see the power of the employer, watch what happens to senior executives when they leave the big firms they used to run. The masters of the universe become outcasts: no one takes their call. Even CEOs become shadows of themselves once they step down.

Choosing the right firm is fundamental to influence. Choosing a large and prestigious firm is a short cut to personal prestige and influence in the market place. This is reflected in the recruiting season at undergraduate and graduate levels: the top employers in consulting, law and banking are inundated with applications from the best and the brightest. They are like the moths attracted to the light. They all fervently believe that they are better and brighter than the rest of the best and the brightest. Slowly, they discover the relentless logic of the career pyramid. If there is one partner for every 25 employees, then even with 10% growth a year, just one in ten of the graduates will make partner inside ten years. Nine out of ten will be disappointed, or will come up with elaborate reasons around how they had always really wanted to start a vegan farm in Vermont. That puts the challenge of influence and power into perspective. If you join the large and prestigious firm, you will need to do more than be bright and work hard to succeed. The art of influence becomes essential: to stand out, to make things happen, to have a claim to fame and to find the right assignments and opportunities in order to succeed.

Global firms would appear at first glance to give the widest range of opportunities. To some extent, they do. But global firms are rarely global: not all nations are equal in a global firm. In global firms, the influential place is the home nation. French, Japanese, American, Indian and Chinese firms may hire plenty of foreigners. Some may be promoted to senior positions. But the overwhelming

> not all nations are equal in a global firm

weight of power is with the home country nationals. This is routinely reflected in the choice of CEO, who normally comes from the home nation. Exceptions, such as Carlos Ghosn (Nissan) or Howard Stringer (Sony) are notable precisely because they are exceptions to the rule.

Home country bias also causes serious problems lower in the organisation. Global teams rarely work as well as they are meant to. Part of the problem is about power. As one Welsh worker with a French company explained: 'I never see the team leader: all the decisions seem to be made over there. I try double guessing what is expected but it is a waste of time. They don't trust us and we don't trust them.' The place of power is clear: it is nearly always with the home nation. Choose your employer well.

Choice of function

As this book first went to press, P&G announced that Robert McDonald was taking over from AG Lafley as the new CEO. I did not have to guess what his background was. I knew what his background had to be. The only source of power and influence at P&G is marketing and brand management. He had to have come from that route. A quick check showed that this was the case. His marketing career had taken him from North America to Japan and Asia, giving him the global outlook which P&G wanted from the new CEO. The only way to the top at P&G is through brand management. Even at the lowest levels of the firm, this truism is keenly felt: it is the brand groups which drive most of the critical business decisions across the firm on a day to day basis. Manufacturing, sales, R&D, finance, logistics and HR all have vital roles to play. But it is clear that the brands are in the driving seat. If you want power and influence at P&G, joining brand management is a smart move. True to the rule of home country bias, both AG Lafley and McDonald are US citizens: P&G may be global, but it is clear where power lies: in America and in marketing.

In many other firms, the choice of function is not so clear cut. In professional service firms, the nature of power and influence is constantly shifting in response to the market: one industry group or service line will grow rapidly and another shrink. The managers in the growing business all look like heroes; the managers in the

> power follows the money and money follows the client

shrinking businesses get to wear the dunce's cap. Power follows the money and money follows the client: if cash is king then the client is the emperor. The ideal place to be is in a small business unit which is about to grow rapidly. This is much easier said than done.

3 Claims to fame: build your personal platform

Old Uncle Harry had a good war. As he recounted his various tales of the war it became clear that he had, single handed, defeated Nazism (with perhaps a little help from the Russians, Americans and that nice Mr Churchill). The truth was a little more mundane: he had been in the supply corps and never got too close to the action. But that was never going to stop him telling a good tale or two. Harry's claim to fame lasted to his dying day and had served him very well by impressing prospective employers and girlfriends.

A good claim to fame can make a person or an organisation. Tom Peters is a superstar on the corporate speaking circuit. His original claim to fame was to have been a co-author of *In Search Of Excellence*. That is now a widely unread book which languishes in the lower reaches of the Amazon rankings. Even though the original platform is past its sell-by date, it has served its purpose: it has given Tom Peters the chance to build his speaking career.

Similarly, Microsoft benefits from a success platform which has now disappeared. When IBM entered the PC market it was the dominant force in mainframes. It was expected to set the standard in the PC market as well. It happened to choose a start up run by Bill Gates to provide the operating system for its computer. The result is that Microsoft became the de facto standard operating system for all PCs. IBM exited the PC business in 2005 when it completed the sale of its PC division to Lenovo. Microsoft's original platform disappeared, but it still retains a 90% share of the market for desktop operating systems. The mystery of a good platform is that it works even after it has disappeared.

Most of us are not going to publish a best seller, become a corporate speaking superstar or to grab 90% of a global market. But we still need our claim to fame if we are to make our mark. The need for a claim to fame is becoming more important as organisations become flatter and more confusing. One life insurance company manages to have five dimensions to its matrix: products, channels, geographies, customers and functions. Most human beings struggle with more than three dimensions. Even actuaries struggle with five. In complex firms it is easier to hide and even harder to shine. No one knows who was really responsible for what. This matters. If you are just another grey face in cubicle land, it is hard to have influence or power. If you have a claim to fame, you get noticed more and you find more opportunities come your way.

> in complex firms it is easier to hide and even harder to shine

The power of the claim to fame became clear at promotion time. I was tasked with running the promotions commission. There were 30 promotions to hand out among 50 nominees: officially we were told there was no limit. Never trust company propaganda. This meant that there were going to be 20 desperately disappointed people. Firing people is easy relatively: by the time it gets to that stage, both sides recognise the inevitable. Disappointing good people who have worked hard and achieved much is far worse. We sifted through the promotions packages. They were all eulogies of unstinting praise to the extraordinary success of each individual. They were, in other words, a pack of lies. Each pack was an attempt by a boss to fulfil a promise made to a team member: 'Work hard and I will get you promoted.'

In the end, we had to ask ourselves three questions:

1 Who is sponsoring the candidate? (Are the sponsors credible and trustworthy?)

2 What is our personal experience of the candidate?

3 What is the candidate's claim to fame?

The sponsorship question leads back to the influential people principle: you need a powerful sponsor. The personal experience question leads back to the influential places question: it is much easier to make a positive impression if you work in proximity to the people who will decide your career. It is also possible to make a negative impression more easily. The final question was the decider: what was the candidate's claim to fame?

A claim to fame could be more or less anything. One person had become the company expert in the arcane art of building financial business cases for IT projects in UK life assurance companies. It was arcane, but valuable. He got promoted. Another person was notable because she always volunteered to help out with discretionary effort, and she always delivered. She got promoted. Another had been sent to Cumbria on a small, messy project and had turned it into a large and successful project. He got promoted.

4 Agenda control: have a plan

People are busy. We seem more stressed and stretched than ever. Every day there are more challenges and crises to deal with. We need to respond to customers, competitors, colleagues and top managers. The last thing we all need is the chance to do more: we already have too much to do, thank you very much.

The problem of stress and overwork is a wonderful opportunity for influential managers. There are countless opportunities to quietly take control: most people will be delighted that you are taking a problem away from them. They are not just giving you a problem; they are giving you an opportunity to build your influence. Controlling the agenda is a powerful platform from which you can grow your influence.

Taking control gracefully, as opposed to having a power battle, is based on three requirements:

1   Find the right opportunity.

2   Strike early.

3   Move centre stage.

I discovered all three of these rules by accident as a young researcher in the British Parliament. My boss was an MP and responsible for economic and industrial policy. He decided the party needed a new economic and industrial policy. This was not strictly true. The party did not need a new policy: he needed a new policy to show that he was doing something. So he assembled a group of very important people to advise him. They all sat round a table and pontificated for an hour or two. I was gently ignored: I was far too young to be capable of thinking or speaking. Towards the end of the meeting, I made the only contribution I could: I offered to summarise the meeting for them. They were delighted: that was an administrative chore which was beneath their dignity. I did not realise it at the time, but a well chosen administrative chore can be an administrative coup.

> a well chosen administrative chore can be an administrative coup

Back at the office I looked at my scrawled notes. All the grand people had said grand things, but there was no conclusion or direction to any of the comments. So I wrote what I thought would be a good industrial and economic policy, taking care to include one or two comments from each grandee. I then circulated the summary, drawing each recipient's attention to their contribution. They were delighted to see that one of their ideas was getting into the policy document. A couple of revisions later, the policy was agreed. It was, by accident, my policy. Two years later, the whole party imploded: I like to think that it was not my fault.

Let's call up the slow motion replay and see what happened:

- **Find the right opportunity**. Working on the party's economic and industrial policy was better than responding to constituents' housing worries.

- **Strike early**. There are always moments of uncertainty when it is not clear who is going to do what. There is a void waiting to be filled, so fill it. Someone needs to step up and volunteer to solve the problem, lead the analysis, summarise the meeting or take the next steps. The first person to raise their hands, cough, catch the eye of the chairperson or even raise an eyebrow is the person who volunteers. Normally, everyone else will be delighted that they have dodged extra work.

- **Move centre stage**. Offering to facilitate, take notes or summarise sounds tedious and a bit like hard work. It is. But it also puts you centre stage. The facilitator controls the direction of the conversation; the summariser controls the output of the meeting. Anyone can do this at any level.

Taking notes is not the only way to take control. There are always tasks which no one else wants to do; they are too busy and the task is too difficult. That is the void waiting to be filled. Most times, it makes sense to leave the void well alone. If it is a low value task, you simply add to an overcrowded agenda. If it is an opportunity which gives you the chance to shine, strike early and volunteer. Two examples will make the point.

We were setting up a charity. There was a huge amount to do: fund raising, finding staff, building our operations. Fortunately, a kind businessman volunteered to do the tedious work of liaising with lawyers and the Charity Commission to set up the legal structure. It was bureaucracy we were pleased to delegate. And at that moment we lost control of the charity. He used the legal process to install himself as chairman and his friends as trustees. Once installed, there was no way of removing them. They were useless and nearly killed the charity. He filled the void and took control.

The second example took place in a dire company meeting, the sort which all executives have to endure from time to time. Budgets for the following year were being agreed. Head office staff were like rottweilers. They attacked every increase in spending from the operating units. Finally, they got up and announced an increase of 40%, or $35 million, in their own head office budget. There was stunned silence. At the first objection, the COO smiled thinly. 'Well,' he said, 'If anyone thinks we can spend less, they are welcome to come to head office and prove it to us.' No one was foolish enough to take on the power and might of head office: that is a death wish. Well, nearly no one. There is always one person with more courage than sense. I raised my hand. The void had been filled and I had volunteered for the death wish project of cutting head office budget and making enemies of every power broker in the company. Be careful which opportunities you take on.

Summary

There are four main ways of building a power base for the influential manager:

1 Borrow power: influential people.

2 Go where the power is: influential places.

3 Build your reputation: have a claim to fame.

4 Control the agenda: have a plan.

All of this amounts to a BFO: a blinding flash of the obvious. Like much of the art of management it is not a deep secret known only to a few wizards of the art. It is common sense: common sense is in short supply in many workplaces. If you can apply these principles you will already start to acquire influence. As ever, applying common sense in the messy, ambiguous, shifting world of management is not easy.

> common sense is in short supply in many workplaces

Chapter 10

Turning dreams into reality

nfluence is not just about being influential. There is a purpose to influence: it is about making things happen. More to the point, it is about making great things happen that you could not achieve alone. It is about helping you make your dreams come true, to achieve more than you ever thought possible.

From the outset, this book has been about the practice of influence: it is not a theory. It is practice which has enabled me to start six national charities, create a bank and help 250 ex-offenders start their own business. I will also ensure that $2 trillion of US and UK government debt is eliminated from their national accounts. That will take a little longer, because the idea is heretical today. Within five years it will be orthodoxy.

Your dreams and ambitions will be different. But your biggest obstacles are not about lack of money, lack of contacts or lack of support. The biggest obstacle to success is in your own head. Here are some of the demons which lurk in my mind every time I start a new adventure:

- I can't do it, it's far too big.
- If it fails, I will look really stupid to family, friends and colleagues. Again.
- If it is such a good idea, why has no one done it before?
- I have no idea how to start.
- I don't have the time for this.

- Other people know more about this than I do.
- Someone will steal my idea if I start talking about it.
- There are some horrible downsides and risks to this idea.

Ultimately, all of these objections come down to one problem: 'I don't really believe in myself and my idea.' You have to slay these demons. Otherwise you will go into your old age always thinking about what might have been, could have been. Worse, you may see someone else take 'your' idea and make it a success. They will be living your success, and you will be living with your regret. That is not worth it.

So how do you overcome these demons, short of going to a shrink every week or listening to motivational audio books? These are not fates to be encouraged. Put simply, you need a method. You need something which you can use in a risk free manner while slowly building up and exploring your idea. Your idea may be for a great new business or charity, or it may be something which can improve the organisation where you work. Whichever it is, I use a simple method which I call IPM: Idea, People, Money.

With IPM, you do not need to be courageous and take huge risks in pursuit of your dream. IPM follows the principle of incremental commitment: you build your dream step by step. If you find that there is a fatal flaw in your idea, IPM allows you to exit gracefully and fight another day.

It may seem that you need courage to chase your dream. I discovered that courage is not necessary. It was a lesson I learned from a fire chief. I asked him how he found people who had the courage to go into burning buildings and rescue people in hazardous environments. The fire chief looked at me in disbelief.

'I do not want courageous people,' he said indignantly. 'Courageous people do stupid things and get killed. I want well trained people who will get the job done.' He then explained how he used the principle of incremental commitment in his training programme.

Rookie firemen would first learn to ascend a small ladder safely, and to extinguish small fires. Slowly, the size of the ladder, the size of the fire and the hazards they faced would increase in training. Each step would be a natural and simple step. No courage was required. Eventually, dealing with a major blaze would seem like routine work: routine to the firemen, courageous to you and me.

The same principle works in chasing your dream. Do not jump into the blazing fire of entrepreneurial endeavour without preparation. Incremental commitment is a principle which works both as an influencing tool and as a way of chasing your dream. You do not need to take big risks. IPM lets you build your way to success in simple steps.

The IPM agenda

Each successful idea has followed the same pattern: IPM. That stands for Idea, People and Money. And they come in that order. The unsuccessful start ups put money first. For instance, at one stage a few of us decided to make a fortune by revolutionising the insurance industry. It was a great idea for a dozy industry which needs shaking up. But we spent so much time arguing over who should get what share of the eventual pot, that we ended up mistrusting each other and the idea flopped before it started. It is natural but lethal to start with the money.

The idea

Always start with the idea: a good idea will attract great people, attract the investment and eventually make money. The bigger the idea, the better: it is easier to attract people and investment to a big idea than it is to a small idea.

Telling people to have a good idea is like telling them to be witty and inspirational. It is not easy. So how do you have a good idea? Fortunately, there are a number of tried and tested ways of coming up with winning ideas, as follows.

1 **Copy an idea**. This is really simple. Teach First came from listening to the radio in San Francisco: they were talking about a great project (Teach For America) which gets top graduates to teach in inner city schools. I rang Wendy Kopp, the founder of Teach For America, and asked if we could adapt the idea for the UK. The rest was history, and a lot of hard work. In the same way, Ryanair became the largest airline in Europe by adapting the SouthWest airlines model from the United States: the idea was in full view of everyone and it was working. Ryanair was the first to have the sense to copy it.

2 **Solve a problem**. I was really angry with the banks: they were lazy, inefficient, ripping off medium size businesses with poor service, high prices and obscene profits. Brilliant! That meant we had to be slightly less lazy and inefficient, with slightly better prices and we could build a profitable business bank. Similarly, James Dyson saw that vacuum cleaners lost suction which made them work poorly. He solved the problem and built a fortune. In your own industry you should be able to spot inefficiencies, gaps and nonsense. Don't grumble about it, do something about it.

3 **Listen to your customers, suppliers, partners**. They will tell you what they want, what they are missing. The bank idea did not come from brilliant analysis. It came from listening to business people I was dealing with: they all complained about their banks. And they all knew exactly what they wanted. They designed the bank for me.

Hopefully, you now have several great ideas for your organisation. But how do you know that they really are great? How do you know that they are not fatally flawed? A little bit of desk research will weed out the worst ideas quickly. But do not disappear into a darkened room for months doing research on your idea. There is a better way of developing it. Talk to people.

Talking to people accelerates your idea greatly. By talking about it, you will achieve three things. You will:

1 **Find out any flaws in the idea fast**. But be careful: there are plenty of people out there who like to prove they are clever by showing that your idea is dumb (and that therefore they must be smart). They are corrosive of confidence and self-belief. Listen to them anyway. They may have a genuinely good concern, or they may simply be trying to show they are smart.

2 **Develop your idea fast**. The hallmark of a good idea is that each time you hear an objection to it, you find the solution and the idea becomes even better. Again, find the solution by talking to more people: don't do it all yourself.

3 **Find out who you want on your team, and find backers and supporters for your idea**. The negative types who find problems, not solutions, rule them out of your success. But you will find enthusiasts: these are the people you should cultivate and encourage. Bring them close into your idea and your emerging team.

Typically, people have two sorts of objections to sharing their idea with other people. First, they are worried that other people will steal their idea. There is always that risk. But in practice, other people have their own lives to lead. They are busy chasing their own dreams and fighting their own fires. Your idea may be entertaining and exciting, but they will not have the energy and passion to develop the idea and pull together the team. They will happily jump on your bandwagon, but stealing your bandwagon is too much effort.

The second objection is that they will look stupid when they share the idea: this is the classic fear of rejection. You can overcome this by using the PASSION principle for the structured conversation. You no longer have to sell your idea: instead you gently explore the idea with a potential partner. Use the PASSION principle well (see Chapter 1), and your partner will be explaining to you how your idea can work, rather than you explaining it to them.

And finally, be bold with your idea. The bolder it is, the more likely you are to make progress. If you have an idea for reducing the amount of paper clips in the office, that is worthy but will be ignored. The bigger the idea, the more people will be interested, and potentially excited. When developing the business bank, I was able to meet CEOs and chairmen of existing banks, because it was a big enough idea to command their attention. If in doubt, be bold.

_____

if in doubt, be bold
_____

People

Venture capitalists rarely back just a great idea. They normally also back a great team. An average idea from a great team is more likely to succeed than a brilliant idea from a weak manager. This is not just how venture capitalists think: it is also how senior managers in your organisation are likely to think as well. They back people even more than they back ideas.

In most of the ventures I have started, I have had no relevant credibility, experience or contacts. So the solution is simple. If you lack personal authority and credibility, borrow credibility from someone else. Find people with credibility, influence and authority who will support your idea. And this is where you need to dance a little. Do not expect powerful and busy people to drop everything and put their reputations on the line to support you: that will not happen.

Again, go back to the principle of incremental commitment. Ask for a small 'give'. When we started Teach First, we knew we could not get big companies to fund us immediately. Instead, we simply asked them if they would sign a pledge which said that Teach First was a good idea. Most businesses were delighted to be let off so lightly: they all signed. Soon enough we were able to produce brochures which showed that we had the support of many of the top businesses in the UK. That created confidence and gave us legitimacy: suddenly, government ministers were willing to talk to us and other top businesses wanted to be associated with us. The bandwagon started to roll.

Within your own organisation, you can follow a similar approach. Don't ask for everything all at once. Ask Finance to sign off on the financial side of things: do not ask them to evaluate the whole idea, because they may raise other concerns. If that is too much to ask, then get Finance to evaluate the possible benefits of your idea, without any of the costs. You then have a prize to dangle in front of everyone else, a prize which is worth fighting for. Do the same with other departments: ask for partial approval of one aspect of the idea. Build your coalition slowly. Keep any disagreements in private: don't let opposition become public because then it becomes hard to shift. But make sure any partial agreements are widely publicised. Build your bandwagon of support, so that success seems inevitable. Keep your doubts to yourself.

You need the right people to support you. In this context, the right people means a mix of six sorts of person:

1 **Your sponsor**. Your sponsor might be your boss. For a project it may be some other power broker. The sponsor may not be involved much, but they have the power to help you get the right team and the right budget. They will also clear any political blockages for you. If your boss or sponsor can not do this for you, then you need to find a better and stronger sponsor.

2 **Your team members who work directly for you**. You may have control over them, but you need to move beyond control to building commitment. You need to become the leader they *want* to follow, not the leader they *have* to follow.

3 **Technical buyers**. These people are not on your team and you do not control them. They can not even make things happen. But they can stop things happening. They have the power to say no. They may exist in legal, finance, health and

safety, compliance. Work with them from an early stage; respect them and bring them on board. They may have absurd demands, but your job is to get them to say yes, not to change the nature of their job for them.

4 **Influencers**. Look out for these people. They may not have a strong formal role, but they will be trusted as an impartial source of advice. They may be old timers who have seen it all before, or they may be in staff functions like planning. They can work the grapevine, or perhaps they whisper in the ear of the CEO.

5 **Gatekeepers**. These are the people who can open the doors to the high and the mighty. The good news is that they can offer you a short cut. The bad news is that they will often demand their pound of flesh in return. In the worst cases, they will effectively hold you hostage: 'do this for me before I give you access'. And then you find they can't get you access anyway. Always have a Plan B: never rely on one gatekeeper alone.

6 **Coach**. Find someone who will coach you and support you. This could be your sponsor. Ideally it is someone whom you can trust and who has eyes and ears in the rest of the organisation. A problem shared is a problem halved, and there are always problems which are difficult to share with team members or your boss.

With each of these people, use the principles of influence to engage them. As you talk to them, you will find they naturally select themselves. Some select themselves as potential team members, others deselect themselves. And it is very obvious which are which. The key difference is how they deal with problems. Even enthusiasts may see problems with your idea, but they will immediately start searching for solutions to the problems they identify. They are the people you want on your team. Then there are the cynics who revel in finding problems and ooze condescension and superiority. Count them out of your potential team.

The right team for you is not just about skills. You also need a team with the right values. As one CEO put it: 'I hire most people for their technical skills, and fire most for their values'. You can train skills, you can not train values. Make sure that whoever you enlist to support you shares your values and beliefs.

Money

If you have a great idea and a great team, the money will follow.

If the money does not follow, look again at the quality of your idea and your team. The chances are that something is missing.

This sounds like it trivialises the money challenge. And to some extent it does. Every start-up goes through at least one or two near-death experiences, and they are usually to do with lack of money. When I was sent to run a business in Japan, I found a business with no sales, no prospect of any sales and no existing customers. But it had a lot of bills which could not be paid. It was dead in the water. But most of the team was good, and we had a good business idea. We survived.

If you look at the history of many business successes, they are stories of David taking on Goliath and winning. FedEx, Toyota, Dell, Ryanair, Sky and Dyson all started with nothing and they were taking on giants such as UPS, Ford and GM, IBM, British Airways, BBC and Hoover. They were nuts: they did not have the money or muscle to win against such giants. And yet they all succeeded. In each case, they had a genuinely outstanding business idea with which to challenge the incumbents. A great idea beats the dull weight of money every time.

> a great idea beats the dull weight of money every time

There is no simple formula for finding the money. A business start-up is different from a charity which is different from finding funding within your own organisation. But there are some basic principles to follow:

- Size the prize, which is ideally a financial benefit if you need investment. Keep dangling the prize in front of everyone: if the prize is big enough then it is worth overcoming significant hurdles to reap the reward. The prize is the rock on which you base all your arguments, so make sure it is credible.

- Build your coalition of support. Borrow credibility and influence from others, so that your idea looks credible.

- Use the principles of influence to build support: follow the PASSION structure of conversations, ask for incremental commitments.

- Remember that 'no' is simply a prelude to a 'yes'.

The last principle is very important. You will suffer multiple rejections. Don't get emotional, don't get upset. That is the way things are. If you have multiple potential funders (for a charity or new business) then the real losers are the people who have failed to back your great idea. If you have only one potential funder (the CEO of your organisation) then be ready to try again. But either way, make sure you learn from each rejection so that you can make your next approach stronger. You should never leave a decision making meeting without understanding *why* the decision was made: answering the question 'why' gives you the tools to make your proposal even stronger.

When we asked for funding for Teach First we had one major funder who had to agree: the government. At our big meeting, the Minister came in and killed the idea stone dead. All the business people got up and left the meeting muttering things like 'jolly good try...hard luck old chap...maybe another time'. All we could hear was the sound of their feet retreating into the distance. It was a near-death experience.

But we used the principle that 'no' is simply a prelude to a 'yes'. We asked the remaining civil servants why the Minister said no, when we had been told to expect yes. This time we listened properly. So when they said that the idea was risky, we understood that the real risk was that our idea was too good: it would show that existing programmes were costly and ineffective. And that would embarrass the Minister. For a civil servant, it is better to waste taxpayers' money than it is to embarrass your Minister. Embarrassing your Minister is a career limiting move. So we reworked the idea. We took great care to show that it would not affect existing programmes and the Minister would look great. The civil servants purred with delight and the Minister approved the programme. Of course, it did show existing initiatives were a waste of money, and they were quietly killed off.

Plan A and Plan B

When pursuing your IPM agenda, it is natural to imagine a glide path which is nice and smooth and leads to a safe landing for your idea. Life is not like that. Generals say that no plan survives the first contact with the enemy. And no idea survives its first contact with reality. Everything changes. Heraclitus, the leading pre-Socratic philosopher, went further:

> no idea survives its first contact with reality

you can never swim in the same river twice, because everything is in a constant state of flux.

You need to be flexible, and you always need a Plan B.

In practice, that means you should go into every meeting knowing your desired outcome, and with a back up. Whatever the outcome is, there should be some next steps. Even if your idea is rejected, you should understand why. And then ask directly, 'Let's meet again when we have dealt with your concerns fully.' If you leave the meeting without a next step, it is very hard to build any momentum again.

Plan B means you should also have alternative routes to success. If one person does not help, know at least one or two other people who could help instead. Once you become dependent on one person, your risk goes through the roof. You become a slave, not a partner, to the person you depend on. It is a very uncomfortable position to be in.

Crises and opportunities

So far, we have assumed that you are chasing a 'green field' dream: an idea which is completely new and original, at least in the context of where you are working. These ideas are often exciting, but they are difficult to put into practice. By definition, a new idea is one that no one is working on; there is no budget for it; no one supports it to start with; your new idea will create extra work, require extra resources and cut across existing agendas and priorities. And most people are risk averse, which means that they see new ideas as risky: they will upset the existing way of doing things. No wonder it is hard to build support for a new idea.

Fortunately, you do not need to have a brilliant new idea or leave your organisation to stake your claim to fame. In most organisations, there is a constant stream of opportunities for you to stake your claim to fame. Occasionally, the opportunity is presented gift wrapped for you. Beware of such gifts: the gift may be less attractive than the wrapping. I was gifted the opportunity to take a one way ticket to Japan, where our business was in chaos. Or perhaps you are offered the opportunity to take on a 'challenging' budget, or new business opportunity. 'Challenging' is business speak for mission impossible.

More often, your opportunity will come carefully disguised as a crisis. Fortunately, organisations are crisis prone: suppliers let you down; the competition mess you up; customers want everything by yesterday; key staff disappear and genuine crises blow up out of nowhere. These can be perfect opportunities to stake your claim to fame.

There is always a moment, at the start of each crisis, where no one is quite sure what to do. No one knows who should take the lead.

Some colleagues will be denying that there is a problem; others will be busily trying to figure out who should take the blame if things get really ugly. This is the moment of uncertainty when the real leaders emerge: they take control and lead the way to a solution. Offer to sort the problem out and your bosses and colleagues will be relieved: that is one less thing for them to worry about. The bigger the problem, the more opportunity you have to make a name for yourself.

Crises accelerate your career: you will succeed fast or you will fail fast. You will achieve visibility to top management well beyond your daily responsibilities. It pays to know how to deal with crises well.

> crises accelerate your career: you will succeed fast or you will fail fast

Let's start with how *not* to deal with crises:

- **Deny the problem**. Crises do not sort themselves out. They have a habit of getting uglier all the time.

- **Find someone to blame**. Passing the buck may help your short-term survival, but it creates a poisonous fog of politics and ensures you acquire enemies for the future.

- **Get angry, frustrated or depressed**. You will be judged as much on how you are as what you do. And emotions are infectious: if you start getting angry or frustrated, others will follow you. That is not productive.

It may seem obvious that these are ineffective ways of dealing with crises. They also happen to be very common ways in which people react to crises. Even when a pitfall is obvious, people still fall into the pit.

Here is how you can deal with a crisis well:

- **Recognise the problem early**. The sooner you deal with it, the easier it is to sort out.

control: step up to the mark. Offer solutions, not
ms. Have a plan. Or at least, build a plan fast with your
colleagues.

- **Focus on what you can do, not on what you can't do**. Build
  momentum, build confidence. There may be only one small
  thing you can do (call an emergency meeting, for instance):
  if that is the only thing you can do, do it. Don't worry about
  things you can't control, because you can't control them.

- **Find support**. This is the IPM agenda: find people who can
  help. Don't be the lone hero, because lone heroes are the ones
  who die first.

- **Overcommunicate**. There will be fear, uncertainty and
  doubt. Be clear and consistent, have a simple story to tell about
  what you will do.

- **Be positive**. You will be remembered as much for how you
  behaved as for what you did. Be the role model for others to
  follow. Wear the mask of confidence and purpose, even if you
  feel doubt and fear behind your mask.

- **Avoid blame, even if there is blame to be apportioned**.
  Leave that to the post mortem. Create a culture of action and
  cooperation, not analysis and blame.

- **Be generous**. Do not hog the credit: be lavish in your praise of
  everyone who helps. By giving praise, you are also showing that
  you were in control and taking the lead.

Summary

Influence is not an end in itself. It is a means to an end. Only
you can decide what you want to achieve. But if in doubt, be
ambitious. Most of us are limited not by our ability, but by our
ambition: we lack enough self-belief to make our dreams come
true. Great leaders are not modest. Alexander the Great lived in a
tinpot state on the edge of ancient civilisation. Before the age of 30
he had conquered the known world and beyond. We all remember
Alexander the Great: no one remembers his uncle Alexander the

Reasonable. When you accept reason, you accept failure: there are always reasons why something can not be done, why the deadline is impossible, why costs can not be cut any more.

You do not need to take wild risks to follow your ambition. Use the IPM model, use incremental commitment, the PASSION structure of conversations. Find the right opportunity or crisis to make your mark.

Ambition for your company, your team and then for yourself is good. A simple form of ambition is to ask: 'How does this look to bosses two levels above me?' If it makes no impression on their agenda, you are not making an impact. I learned this lesson when I first presented a promotions plan to the board. I was ready for all the questions about costs, redemption levels, supermarket support, logistics and the rest of the detail I had been sweating over. The board was not interested. They wanted to know things like: will this cannibalise other brands? Will it improve or dilute our brand equity? Can we replicate this internationally? They were big questions to which I had no clue. I had been thinking at the wrong level: they wanted strategy and all I had was detail.

When you are ambitious you set an agenda which resonates across the organisation, not just in your own silo. In this sense, influence is like your credit card. Once you go beyond your formal limit of credit (authority and influence) and you can cope with it,

> influence is like your credit card

you get invited to extend your credit (authority and influence) even further. Bigger and larger opportunities come your way.

Being ambitious means being unreasonable, selectively. You have to push and stretch your team to achieve more than they believe is possible. This is not being mean to them: it is only by stretching them that they develop new skills and new capabilities. There are, clearly, limits to the art of unreasonable management. Unreasonable management should not be about hectoring, finger wagging, and demeaning people. To be unreasonable and ambitious effectively, managers should:

- Be firm about the goals, flexible about the means.
- Support and enable the team at all points.
- Give the team a sense of control: the difference between pressure and stress is control. If I have pressure and no control over my fate, I feel stress. If I feel pressure but remain in control I will stretch and develop.
- Read the warning signals: if the team shifts from pressure to stress, lead them straight back down the mountain to their comfort zone. Let them reacclimatise before leading them back again.

To be influential, managers must make a difference, and that requires ambition.

Part 2

Influence in practice

Chapter 11

Moments of truth

There are moments when we all see power ebbing and flowing between people. They are moments when people move from obscurity to centre stage. In some cases, they are centre stage and implode in spectacular fashion. Months and years of work can suddenly pay off or get lost.

Most of these moments of truth are predictable. We can prepare for them, even if we can not predict exactly when and where the moment of truth will happen. Classic moments of truth include getting the right or wrong assignment; making a presentation to top management which flies or falls; going to meetings where essential decisions are made for or against your interests. Every career is full of such moments. We have to learn to make the most of each one of them.

In practice, there are seven moments of truth all managers must prepare for if they are to build and sustain influence:

1 Assignments.
2 Taking over a new team or role.
3 Budgets.
4 Meetings.
5 Presentations.
6 Conflicts.
7 Crises.

We have covered crises at length in the previous chapter. Influential managers learn to turn crises into opportunities. And they learn to turn the other moments of truth to their advantage as well. Because crises have been covered already, this chapter will focus on the remaining six moments of truth.

Assignments

The path to leadership is often a random walk of experience. With good bosses and assignments we learn and grow fast. And then we find a boss from the dark side and the assignment from hell. Suddenly, survival is success. If we are to build our careers and our influence, then we have to have the right boss, with the right assignment in the right organisation. Finding this magic combination is our responsibility. If we leave our career direction to the tender mercies of the HR department then we have to hope to get lucky. But hope is not a method and luck is not a strategy. If you delegate your career to HR, you will discover that 'career' is both a noun and a verb. When you let others take control, career becomes a verb which accurately describes your random walk to the future.

> hope is not a method and luck is not a strategy

Three simple tests will tell you if you have made the right choice of boss, firm and assignment:

- Will I learn and have the right experience?
- Will I succeed?
- Will I enjoy it?

Will I have the right experience?

In theory we should learn from schools, courses, textbooks and lectures. In practice, managers learn from experience. We see someone mess up, and quietly make a note not to do the same thing. We see someone do something very well, and might try it ourselves. Books and courses tell us what we should do; experience shows what actually works. So it is your most vital career tool.

The key experience test is to ask yourself: 'What skills will I need to flourish one or two levels further ahead in my career?' That means you need to learn new things, rather than become ever more expert at your current job. Expertise may be well paid, but it is not the high road to the top. As careers progress, technical skills become decreasingly important. Instead, people and political skills become essential: the subtle arts of influence become more important the further you progress in an organisation. In practice, this requires gaining experience of working across the organisation, not just within your own department. You have to push beyond your comfort zone. As you deal with other departments, you have to deploy influencing, political and people skills in abundance: by definition, you can not tell other departments what to do – you have to influence and persuade them.

Will I succeed?

The obvious questions to ask here are:

- Will I have the right team?
- Will I have the right budget?
- Will I have achievable goals?
- Will I have a supportive boss?
- Do I have the right skills?

It pays to play hardball before you accept the assignment. The moment you accept the assignment, all your negotiating power has disappeared. Playing hardball can be done constructively. No one wants an assignment to be set up to fail: your negotiation should be about how to set the assignment up for success. Everyone should want a positive outcome. Keep pushing until you are satisfied. You do not need to have changed the entire team before you start, but you need to make sure you have the right to change it fast after you start.

The success question leads to a huge trap. The best way to assure success is to take on an easy assignment which does not stretch you. That is a passport to mediocrity and under-achievement. You need courage to stretch yourself. So the extra success question you should ask is: 'Will my success be noticed at least two levels above me?' If only your boss knows of your success, then you are invisible: that is not a good way to build influence or to lay a claim to fame.

By focusing on success which is visible across the organisation, you stretch yourself and you force yourself to learn the skills which you will need for the future.

Will I enjoy it?

I am yet to meet a CEO who does not enjoy what they do. Of course, many CEOs are professional grumblers: they grumble about all the air miles they do, the tax they pay and the burdens they have to bear. That is their way of boasting about how much they travel, how much they earn and how important they are. They grumble, and love every moment of it. Equally, I know of no sports person or artist who dislikes what they do, despite the endless hours of tedious practice.

> you only excel at what you enjoy

Put simply, you only excel at what you enjoy. The management career is a marathon, and it has plenty of bleak and challenging moments. Anyone can sustain enthusiasm for a day or two. The challenge is to sustain enthusiasm year after year after year. If you can do that, you can overcome all the 'slings and arrows of outrageous fortune' which managers, like Hamlet, have to endure. You have to find something you genuinely enjoy doing.

There is a trap with this question. Most people do not leave their organisation: they leave their boss. But the corporate carousel keeps on turning. A bad boss today can be replaced by a better boss tomorrow. As a rule, it is better to seek a move within your organisation than to jump to another organisation. The new organisation will put their best face on when trying to recruit you and you may like your new boss. You then move and find that your new organisation still has politics, crises and incompetence; and your new boss may have been replaced by another boss from hell. When head hunters promise you greener pastures elsewhere, remember that it is greenest where it rains most.

Finding the right assignment is easier said than done.

It starts by finding the right employer. If you join a traditional firm which is downsizing every two years, it is harder to progress than if you join a start-up which is growing at 50% per year. But the start up may also go bust next year. So your starting point is to judge your prospective employer as much as they judge you. Only work for a firm which has a source of unfair advantage. The problem with a fair fight is that you might lose it. The only fights worth having in the market are so unfair that you are bound to succeed. In the words of legendary investor Warren Buffet: 'I only invest in firms which any fool can run, because some day some fool will run it.' Only work for a firm which any fool can run, because some day some fool *will* run it.

Within the firm, find the right assignment. Make friends with HR. Keep your ear to the ground. Make yourself useful to bosses at least two levels above: when they have good opportunities, they will keep you in mind. Assume the Harry Potter cloak of invisibility when the death star boss and assignment is looking for victims: make sure you are very busy and very committed elsewhere. When the golden opportunity starts to emerge, make yourself available: offer to put in some voluntary help to get things going, to help the boss. Make yourself part of the fabric of the new opportunity. Don't be naive and rely on HR. Control your destiny, or someone else will.

Taking over a new team or role

Influence and power are closely linked. Influence is about creating informal power which extends beyond your formal authority. Power comes from your formal position, in theory.

But in practice, there are many people in positions of power who are not in control. The classic example was British Prime Minister John Major. He was attacked, by his own side, for 'being in office, not in power'. You can have the title but still not have the power, unless you use it.

> **the first rule of power is use it or lose it**

The first rule of power is use it or lose it. That means taking over properly from day one. Within a month of taking over, everyone on your team, and your colleagues and your bosses will have decided what you are like in your new role. Changing those initial perceptions is hard work: best to get it right first time.

Your agenda for taking over successfully is the same as the agenda for making your dreams come true. It is the IPM agenda: Idea, People and Money. And this is how the agenda works when you take over.

Idea

If we want to be grand, we can call this your vision. But it is no more than your story of what you are going to do in your new role. Your story will have three parts:

1 This is where we are.
2 This is where we are going.
3 This is how we will get there.

If it takes you more than ten seconds to say where you are going, that is too long. The whole story need not be more than 30 seconds. No one will remember the long, sophisticated analysis and 37 point plan that you dream up with your consultants. And if they can not remember it, they can not act on it.

A good idea can be very simple, such as:

- We will focus more on customer service.
- We will improve time to market.
- We will achieve best in class costs.
- We will professionalise the operation.

From one simple statement, a whole battery of initiatives can flow. Your one simple idea can focus the organisation, give it direction and purpose and clarify priorities. Without a simple idea, you will have confusion in your head and in your team.

And if you want to make your vision or idea motivational, make it relevant to each member of your team. Show how they can help achieve the vision you have laid out. If you decide that you want a customer focused organisation, then clearly both the receptionist and the toilet cleaner have an important role to play: they make an impression on customers. Once you have your idea, you need to sell it.

People

Never assume that the team you inherit is the team you have to live with. It will be a mix of the good, the bad and the misplaced. The 'B' team is a recipe for sleepless nights, overwork, worry and stress: they will make mountains out of molehills. Your 'A' team will make molehills out of mountains and will over-deliver. Like any good football manager, one of your key tasks is to build the right team. Some of that comes through training and developing your team; some of it comes from making sure each member of your team is in the right position; much of it comes from bringing the right people into the team from the start.

Expect to restructure your team within a month or so of taking over. If nothing else, this is a good way of showing you are in charge. One new boss of large IT division found herself in charge of eight geographically based power barons, who liked to think that they were kings of Italy, France, Germany, Spain and so on. Within a month she had reorganised around industries (financial services, pharmaceuticals, transport, public sector etc). The reorganisation in theory was about building expertise. In truth, it was an exercise in power. All the power barons were moved into industry sectors, and a couple lost their jobs. Suddenly, she was the all powerful queen of the business and the barons were cowed into obedience. The odd ritual execution has a powerful effect on the survivors. Previously she had not been in control of the barons; within a month everyone knew who the boss was.

Reorganising is a wonderful way to reset the psychological contract with each member of your team. It is a chance to sit down with each one and explain exactly what you expect. Expectations are not just about performance goals: they are also about the way of working. That makes the discussion a two way street: they need to hear what you expect and you need to hear what they expect. If you can listen and act on what you hear, you are likely to build respect and loyalty fast.

Money

Your predecessor may well have left you a few post dated cheques, which you will be expected to honour. He or she may have painted a picture of a unit which is on the brink of success where efficiency and profits will soar. If you live with that, you will live with hell. You need to reset expectations very fast. Search all the cupboards for all the skeletons which have been hidden away. Paint a picture of a unit which is near to total collapse: it is going to take a genius (you) to prevent catastrophe occurring. If your version of events is accepted, then survival is success. Set expectations low and over-deliver.

set expectations low and over-deliver

Expectations of performance and budget are, or should be, linked. Fight hard for the budget you need. How you do that is the subject of the next section.

When you take over, there will be plenty of things to distract you. You will be learning all about your new unit and your new team; you will be learning new skills; you will find yourself sucked into a new routine of reporting and meeting; there will be fires to fight and deadlines to meet. This day-to-day survival can be completely overwhelming when you first start in a new role. Do not get sucked into the frenzy of day-to-day activity. Delegate everything you can to your team: see how they cope. Give yourself time to build your IPM agenda, gain support for it and then act on it. It is the investment of time which will ensure you set yourself up for success.

Budgets

In theory, the budget process is a rational method of allocating resources efficiently across the organisation. In theory, we should not have wars, famine, corruption or people who eat smelly food on public transport.

In practice, the budget process is deeply political. It is the process where each level of management negotiates a contract with the levels above and below. The goals of the negotiation are the mirror opposite of each other depending on your position in the food chain.

When negotiating a budget with your bosses, you should seek to minimise your promises and maximise the resources you are allocated. When setting a budget for teams beneath you, you need to do the opposite: maximise the promises you get and minimise the resources you have to commit.

If you want a year of living in hell, try being macho and accept the 'challenging' budget you are first presented with. All managers should rise to a challenge, in theory. But they should not sign up to a year of chasing lunatic goals with minimal resource.

Ensuring that you have the right budget settlement follows the same principles as influencing any sort of decision. Influencing decisions is clearly a key task of any influencer, and is covered in the next section. For our purposes now, it is enough to note that the budget is a must-fight and must-win battle of the annual corporate calendar: do not leave it to the planners and finance department to seal your fate for the coming year.

Influencing decisions

Business is not a democracy. Decisions are made which affect you and your career, but you do not get to vote on those decisions. That does not mean you can't influence those vital decisions, such as budgets, assignments, team allocations, priorities and more. If you are to have any influence as a manager, you have to know how to influence decisions in your favour.

Surprisingly, this is a very practical area where some very academic research hits the jackpot. Daniel Khanemann won the Nobel Prize for Economics for his work on decision making heuristics: he examined the short cuts people use to make difficult decisions in uncertain situations. To simplify his work massively, here are nine principles which practising managers can put to use.

Anchoring. Is the moon more or less than 25 million kilometres from earth? I have absolutely no idea. But I have just anchored the debate around 25 million. Should next year's budget be cut by 5% or 10%? No idea, but the debate has just been anchored around a cut and the compromise may be around a 7% cut. If you don't like that, then make sure that you anchor the debate for your unit around the question 'should my unit have its budget increased by 15% or 20%?' You anchor the debate by getting your retaliation in first: strike before anyone else does and make your position the one which people fight over. Stake your claim first.

> make your position the one which people fight over

Framing. Would you like to enter a competition where you have a 99.999999% chance of losing? Or would you prefer a competition where you have a chance of winning $10 million for just $1 entry? The two competitions are, of course, the same. Frame the business decision the same way. Faced with a business which was going bust in Japan, I asked my global masters if they would like to invest $4 million in building a profitable Japan business, and avoid the cost and embarrassment of closing down Japan. They agreed, which meant that they agreed to losses of $4 million over three years. I suspect that if I had asked if I could lose or waste $4 million of their money, they would not have been so supportive. 'Investment' is good and 'losses' are bad, even if they are the same thing. Language counts. Frame the decision the way that will get a positive response.

Loss aversion. This is a close companion of framing. Would you invest your pension fund in a policy which offers an 80% chance of doubling your money, but a 20% chance of losing it all? If you could play that game often enough, you would win handsomely. But since you can only play once, most people would duck the offer: the risk of loss is too great. And loss aversion is not just logical: it is also about being made to look like the office fool. In many organisations it is better to be wrong collectively than right individually: if everyone is wrong, then no one will get the blame. When asking for a decision to be made, understand the potential losses and risks for the other person: eliminate the risk and you eliminate the opposition.

Social proof. Welcome to the world of celebrity endorsement: if the sunglasses make the film star look great, then perhaps I will look like a film star as well if I buy them. Fat chance, but hope springs eternal. If you do not have any film stars working in your office, you need another form of endorsement. This is where you have to build a coalition in support of your idea. Build the coalition informally in private one to one meetings, keeping conflict private and making agreement public. Endorsement from senior managers counts, but also make sure you gain the support of finance and all the other functions who can not say yes but have unlimited authority to say no.

Emotional credibility. The papers say there is a crime wave, and I shrug my shoulders and move to the sports page. My neighbour is mugged and suddenly I am worried about crime in the neighbourhood. My house is burgled, and truly crime is out of control. We believe what we experience more than what we read. Do not rely on data and facts alone to make your case. Bring your case to life with stories, examples and the odd killer fact. For instance, we could not persuade a utility company that their service was terrible, despite the consumer research. We did a video of a widow who had been flooded by the water company and left without help for days: the video forced action which argument alone could not achieve.

Restricted choice. Most of us have been in the situation where we go into a store and are overwhelmed by choice. Confused, we leave. Too much choice is dangerous. The more choice you offer, the greater the risk you create: you create the risk in the buyer's mind that they made the wrong choice. If there are 120 different phone packages and tariffs, I can be reasonably confident that I have not found the right one. So a smart influencer restricts the choice: 'You can have this great package (which is absurdly expensive) or this really cheap package (which is totally useless) or this middling package which does what you want at a good price.' Even I can make that choice, on a good day. Restrict choice, make it easy for people to say yes.

Repetition works. All advertisers and dictators know this eternal truth: repetition works. Repetition works. Repetition works. Repetition works. Repetition works. Repetition works. Repetition works. Repetition works. Repetition works. Repetition works. Repetition works. Repetition works. Repetition works. What works? Repetition works! Be persistent: stake your claim time and time again and eventually even the most absurd nonsense can become the received wisdom.

Idleness. I would probably have liked to be a sports star, and an astronaut, and a film star, and a billionaire. And a train driver. All at the same time. But it takes time and effort to achieve these things. And meanwhile, I have the cat to feed before going for a night out. Your colleagues may like you and your idea, but they probably do not like it enough to drop everything they are doing and help you out. So make it easy for them: ask them for the minimum required. Remove any administrative or logistical hurdles for them.

Size the prize. Focus relentlessly on the benefits of your idea. Do you want to improve profits by $2 million a year or not? Focus the discussion on this: lots of people will observe how difficult the task will be, how priorities will have to change, and they will find lots of real and imaginary risks. But keep on coming back to the $2 million prize (or whatever other prize you have identified): it takes a very unusual manager to walk away from a big prize like $2 million a year. By focusing on the prize you change the balance of risk: normally doing anything is risky. But doing nothing (walking away from $2 million) is suddenly huge risk: no manager wants to be the person who walked away from the prize.

Meetings

The head of one French government ministry loved meetings: 'They are a great opportunity to sabotage the agendas of other ministries,' he declared, gleefully. Meetings serve many different purposes, not all of which are about sabotage. But whatever the meeting is, you need to have your own agenda. If you work to someone else's agenda, that is very noble. But if you want to make progress and build influence, you need to know how each meeting can help you with your priorities and agenda.

A successful meeting will answer one, or possibly all three of the following questions:

- What did I contribute?
- What did I learn?
- What did I achieve?

If you can not answer each question positively, the meeting has been a waste of time and you should not have attended. Here is what each question is about.

What did I contribute?

being positive is not a health hazard

A good way of building influence is to be positive, supportive and helpful. Being positive is not a health hazard. Look through the formal agenda before hand and see what and where you can contribute.

What did I learn?

Use every meeting as a learning opportunity: learn about what is happening, learn about the politics, learn about how other people handle themselves well or poorly. But you will only learn if you debrief properly afterwards. The Red Arrows debrief after every training session and to do so well, they suspend the hierarchy. Any rank can criticise any other rank: their collective survival may depend on honest feedback and avoiding future mistakes. If you go to a meeting and only learn, without contributing or achieving anything, then you soon become surplus to requirements. You should learn, but you should do more as well.

What did I achieve?

Occasionally, there will be a formal agenda item for which you are responsible, and it will be clear what you want to achieve. Just as often you will find the most productive part of the meeting is just before the meeting, just after and in the coffee break: this is where you can have an informal conversation with hard to get to executives. An informal conversation is not random: make it structured and purposeful, even if the purpose is only to set up a private meeting at a later date.

If there is a formal decision you need at a meeting, do not leave it to chance. The formal meeting should be no more than a public confirmation of the private agreements you have reached with individuals around the table. If there is one important person at the meeting, like the CEO, who you have not been able to meet, make sure everyone is in support of your proposal. There should be no surprises, if your goal or proposal is important.

We have all been in meetings where we have seen power visibly ebb and flow between attendees: one person goes down in flames, another person quietly gets their way and starts to fly. These are not random outcomes based on luck. With preparation, you will fly not fall.

Presentations

Death by a hundred bullet points to the head is an ugly way to go. But this is the fate which too many presenters inflict on their audiences. These set pieces are where you can achieve great visibility. No one will have seen all your weeks of late nights, but they will see the presentation. These are the moments when you accelerate to success or failure: at promotion time, the bosses will remember your presentation and will have no idea about all the hard work that you put in before hand. Understandably, many people become nervous about making formal presentations.

Presentations are a mixture of style and substance. Style wins. Try to remember a presentation you watched from a year ago: the chances are that you can not remember much of the substance. But you probably can remember the style of the presenter, for better or for worse. So first we will look at style and then at substance.

Style

If you can manage the three Es of presenting, you are likely to do well: enthusiasm, excitement and energy. If you don't project enthusiasm, excitement and energy, no one else will be enthusiastic, excited or energetic for you. You have to lead the way.

As an experiment, try explaining the tax implications of your firm's transfer pricing policy to some friends. See if you fall asleep before they hit you. The chances are, you will not sound very interested. Now try recounting the most exciting legal and decent thing you have done in the last year. The chances are that you will naturally display the three Es: energy, excitement and enthusiasm. Everyone has the natural ability to display the right style. You simply need to transfer your natural ability into the business environment.

To help you transfer the three Es to the stage, visualise what success looks like. If you can, go to the venue before hand, under the guise of checking out the logistics. Then make sure you know exactly how and where you will stand; how you will work the slides, if any. Imagine yourself looking and sounding confident and succeeding. Rehearse success in your mind, and then go and do it.

Substance

If a presentation is important, do it well. That means preparing and rehearsing: it is a show and no actor goes on stage without some rehearsal. Here is how to set yourself up to succeed:

1 **Have a clear goal**. Even if the presentation is simply to report on progress, you should have in mind what a good outcome looks like. Then organise your presentation to achieving that outcome. And when you start your presentation, make sure that your audience knows what the purpose of your presentation is. Most managers are neither psychic nor patient. Be clear about what they should expect.

2 **Tell a story**. It should have a start, a middle and an end. You do not need to be creative. The simplest story is 'this is where

we are, this is where we are going, and here is how and why'.
Watch TV for an evening: ignore the programmes and focus
on the commercials: they all tell stories in 30 seconds or less. If
they can tell a story in 30 seconds, you should be able to tell a
story in five minutes.

3 **Keep it short**. A presentation is not complete when you can
say no more. It is complete when you can say no less. Focus on
what is most important. This is where your story is essential:
have a clear, simple story around which you can hang the key
evidence you should provide.

4 **Dumb slides, smart presenter**. The best thing to do
with PowerPoint is to throw it away: it is boring; it makes
interaction hard; and it locks you into a remorseless logic. But
if you must have slides, make them few and make them simple.
They should do no more than let your audience know where
you are in your presentation. Dumb slides should be brought
to life by your brilliance and insight. The nightmare set up is
to have smart slides, with lots of words and numbers on them,
which the presenter proceeds to read out loud slower than the
audience can read for themselves.

5 **Support assertions with facts**. Words like 'important'
'urgent' and 'strategic' (which is important with bells on) are
meaningless hype. They invite the alert listener to disagree:
it's not important or urgent to me. If you make an assertion,
support it with evidence. Once people start to disagree with
you, they disagree with everything.

6 **Present for the audience, not for yourself**. Work out who
you are presenting to. If you are presenting to 50 people,
there are probably just one or two people you really need to
influence. Focus the presentation on those two people. This
will give your presentation structure, simplicity and focus
which the other 48 people will appreciate as well.

7 **Start well, end well**. I script the first 30 seconds of what I
will say: however nervous I may feel, the script lets me start

confidently and engage the audience. And I have a standard finish for all presentations which leaves people on a high, rather than the limp 'any questions'. Script your finish as well as your start.

8 **Get it right**. One bad number destroys the credibility of the whole presentation: it invites a shooting gallery where everyone is looking for the next error. Equally, spelling errors show a lack of professionalism and reliability.

9 **Focus, focus, focus**. Focus your story to make it simple; focus your message on the people you need to influence; focus your eyes on each individual in the audience. Don't talk to your slides. Don't gaze into the middle distance: you are not addressing the wall at the back of the room. Talk to the audience.

10 **Prepare, prepare, prepare**. The more you prepare and rehearse, the more confident you will be.

Conflicts

Organisations are set up for conflict. This comes as a surprise to most management gurus, but is no surprise to anyone who actually works in an organisation. Conflicts are part of everyday life. Inevitably, different functions have different views of what is important: Marketing and Sales will focus on increasing revenues, while Finance will focus on reducing costs. Different business and geographic units think their own area is most important, and they are competing intensely with each other for the same limited pot of investment. Internal competition is the way in which resources are allocated across the organisation. And this conflict is explicit in multinationals which invite bids from national subsidiaries for the location of the next manufacturing plant or R&D

> the real competition is not in the market place: it is sitting at a desk near you

centre. And of course, all staff compete with each other for the same limited pool of promotions and bonuses. The real competition is not in the market place: it is sitting at a desk near you.

Most of the time, it pays to compete collaboratively: create win–win situations. This is the art of influence. But occasionally, you need to stand your ground. You need to know when to fight and when to compromise. Fortunately, Sun Tsu gives us the answer. Over 2,500 years ago he wrote *The Art of War*. He laid out three conditions which needed to be fulfilled before going to war. These conditions are as true of today's corporate battles as they were in ancient times:

1 Only fight when there is a prize worth fighting for.
2 Only fight when you know you will win.
3 Only fight when there is no other way of achieving your goals.

Only fight when there is a prize worth fighting for

Many corporate battles fail this simple test. The end result of such battles is a loss of trust all round, which is a poor way to build influence. But there are a few battles where there is a prize worth fighting for:

- budgets.
- assignments.
- team formation.

The price of losing or, worse, not even fighting these battles is very high. To succeed, you need the right role with the right budget and the right team. Don't compromise.

Only fight when you know you will win

Generals like to say that most battles are won and lost before the first shot is fired. The same is true of corporate battles. If you have lined up not just all the arguments, but also all the people in support of your position, then you will win. If you are not sure that you will win, then the chances are that you will lose. The saying on Wall Street holds true for any organisation: if you don't know who the fall guy is, you are the fall guy. If you line up all the support properly beforehand, then any rational opposition will melt away before any conflict erupts.

Only fight when there is no other way of achieving your goals

As a rule, it is better to win a friend than to win an argument. You may think you have gloriously routed all your enemies in a famous victory. Rest assured that you now have enemies. They may or may not accept that they have lost the battle, but they certainly will not think they have lost the war. They will bide their time. And in the way corporate world goes, colleagues and even team members can become your boss, or become people on whom you depend heavily. You do not want them to be like a bear with a sore head. If you get to the point where a bare knuckle fight is the only way of achieving your goals, then something has gone seriously wrong with your preparation and influencing skills.

Chapter 12

The myths and reality of influence

Influence: one sin and four myths

The subjects of influence and power are shrouded in mystery and much misunderstood. Although they are essential skills to making things happen in organisations, they are often seen as slightly grubby topics. Managers are comfortable learning about things like accounting and marketing. But learning about influence and power sounds devious, divisive and self-interested. This is unfortunate, because influence and power are central to making organisations work.

One cardinal sin

The bedrock of influence is trust. Most leaders forgive most sins. They know that mistakes happen and disasters occur. They can forgive bad jokes, bad dress and occasionally bad judgement. The one thing most bosses find unforgivable is breach of trust. Once a boss no longer trusts a team member, it is game over. It may take weeks or months, but eventually the boss and team member will part company. Equally, few team members want to work with a boss they do not trust, even if they like the boss personally. Peers have a choice about who they collaborate with: trust plays a central part in that choice.

Without trust it becomes very hard to build alliances, commitment and support across the firm. There is much more to being an effective influencer than trust, but lack of trust is a killer.

Breaking trust is not just a matter of undermining a colleague or a boss. It also includes bad mouthing people behind their backs; breaking perceived promises and commitments; not being honest, or misleading people; failing to support an ally or a boss at a critical moment. All of these are betrayals: even if what you did was technically correct, the sense of betrayal will remain. Shattered trust is like shattered glass: it is very hard to rebuild.

The Machiavelli myth

The art of influence and power is not about Machiavellian politics. Plotting against colleagues, stabbing people in the back and being devious is not the way to gain power and influence. Effective influence is based on trust.

There is a calculating element to influence: you have to know where and when to invest precious time and effort in building your alliances. There is also a ruthless element to influence: knowing when to seize the moment and take control of an agenda. This kind of calculation and ruthlessness is a benign force for the individual and the firm. Everyone benefits when you make the right investments and manage the right agenda. Influence is not, however, about being nice, as we will see in the friendship myth below.

The friendship myth

Influence is not about being liked or making friends. Influence is based on alliances of common interests and trust. Eventually, a professional alliance may become a personal friendship. The goal is to create a productive alliance, not to make a personal friendship. The friendship myth is important because it is natural for people to seek popularity. This simply leads to weakness, pandering to other people's demands and dancing to whatever the mood music of the day might be. Influential relationships are based on partnerships, not friendships. Partners act as equals: they work towards common goals and hopefully share a common understanding of how things should work.

The morality myth

Some people see influence as evil and manipulative; they want influence to have morals and to be a force for good. Influence does not have morals. It is neither moral nor immoral: it is amoral. It is a force for good or a force for evil, depending on who uses it and for what purposes. In other words, influence is as moral as the influencer who uses the skills of influence. Hopefully you will use influence as a force for good; and knowing how influence works you will better resist influence when it is in the wrong hands. That is your choice.

The magic myth

Successful influencers seem to have an aura of magic about them. Everyone wants to get a piece of their magic pixie dust. Like charisma, influence is treated as something you either have or do not have. Because effective influencing is invisible to third parties, it appears to be even more magical and mysterious. The simple message of *How to Influence and Persuade* is that there is no magic to influence: or if there is, this book has decoded the spell. In place of magic there is a series of skills, behaviours and mindsets that all managers can acquire to become influential. As you build these skills you will slowly master the invisible art of influence. Colleagues will start to wonder how you make things happen so easily, how you seem to find the right opportunities, how you turn crises into opportunities and why so many people help you. Whether you share the secret of your magic will be for you to decide.

The practice of influence

We all use mental short cuts for everything: for doing maths, for making decisions, for dealing with people. The short cuts we use are based on our personal experience of what does, and does not work. We rarely, if ever, resort to formal theory to work out how to deal with someone or make a decision. And it is for that reason that this book is not a formal theory: that might be clever, but it would also be useless.

Day to day, I no longer have to think explicitly about the different tools and techniques of influence. They have become second nature. But there are a few short cuts which I always use. These mental short cuts are especially useful when you are in a tight situation and you need to think fast. Some people are natural fast thinkers and thrive under pressure. The rest of us need a few simple short cuts which we can rely on to get us out of a corner.

Here, in completely unscientific fashion, are the short cuts which I use. You may share some of the same short cuts; you may develop other short cuts. The important thing is to make sure that you have a toolkit at your disposal which you can rely on in any situation. My top 20 short cuts are as follows:

1   **Be positive**. You never lose by being positive and enthusiastic. This is particularly important when the outlook is gloomy and the storm clouds are gathering. Bring sunshine, not rain, to the party. Occasionally, influencers and leaders have to wear the mask: even if there is fear, doubt and uncertainty in your heart wear the mask of confidence for the outside world.

2   **Focus on the outcome**. Be relentless in knowing where you want to get to. If you don't know where you are going, you won't get there. You will get lost in the day to day drama of fighting fires: that may be heroic, but it is not productive. Outcome focus is particularly useful in crises when there is plenty of dysfunctional behaviour around: getting lost in the moment, playing the blame game and more. Be the one that rises above the noise and drives to action.

3   **Be ambitious**. The point of influence is not to influence: it is to achieve something. The more ambitious you are, the more there is for people to get excited about. There is a bigger cake to bake and to share.

4 **Strike early**. The earlier you get involved in anything, from new ventures to negotiating budgets or planning meetings, the more influence you have. If you arrive late, you can change the details but not the big picture.

5 **Options**. Always have options. If your career depends on one person, you are a slave. If you have only one desired outcome for the meeting, your fate depends on good fortune. Be flexible; have a back up. You do not need to score a hole in one, but you do need to make progress.

6 **Win–win**. Look at the world through the eyes of the other person: what's in it for them? Everyone has hopes: tap into their hopes. Everyone has fears: make sure your idea does not awaken their demons. Let people have a win; let them have a story which shows they are smart. Don't try to fool people: you may succeed in the short term, but you store up problems for the future.

7 **Focus on interests, not positions**. Positions tend to be win–lose: 'I want a higher/lower price.' Behind every position there are deeper interests. Finding them requires planning, creativity and smart questions. Once you have reframed the challenge from a win–lose position to a set of common interests, you are on the way to success.

8 **Partnership principle**. This is useful in dealing with big bosses and big customers who can be scary. But in truth, they need something from you: you succeed or fail together. Treat them as a partner and they will return the compliment.

9 **Incremental commitment**. Partnership is a two-way street. It pays to be generous of your time, but ask for something in return. The more they give, the more committed they become.

10 **Flatter**. Flattery works. There are plenty of ways of flattering gracefully (see box). This is a good way of building rapport and it makes it far harder for people to argue against you. They will see you as an ally, not an enemy.

11 **The noddy principle**. Find areas of agreement, not disagreement. Argument simply generates more argument and becomes a win–lose. Even if there is only one thing you can agree on, agree on that to start with. Build from there.

12 **Public agreement, private disagreement**. Keep the difficult conversations private. As soon as someone takes a public stand (remember, public is a meeting with three people or more), they will not change their position. They want to save face. Keep disagreement private, but publicise agreements so that the bandwagon starts to roll.

13 **Human nature**. Neither influence nor business is purely rational, whatever the textbooks may say. People are emotional: we have our hopes, fears and dreams. Deal with the person before you deal with the problem.

14 **Build trust**. Friendship is good, but respect is better. Currying favour leads to weakness and you are as popular as your latest favour. Respect lasts, and comes from building trust. Trust comes from being credible (doing as you say) and being aligned (showing you have common interests and goals).

15 **Remove the risk**. The biggest obstacle to progress is risk. Rational risk is easy: it is about money, people and logical problems. The far bigger risk is personal and emotional: 'How will this affect me and my career and how I am seen by my peers and colleagues.' Remove the personal risk, which may only be perception, and the biggest obstacle evaporates.

16 **Plan, plan and plan again**. If it is important do it well.

17 **Two ears, one mouth**. If in doubt, listen. Instead of making smart statements, ask smart questions. Use disclosure and contradiction to encourage more talking; use paraphrasing to show you have understood. Let people talk themselves into agreeing with you and liking you. It works, and takes little effort.

18 **Focus on what you can do, not on what you can't do**. If there is only one thing you can do, do it. Don't worry about things you can't control: all you will do is give yourself an ulcer. By focusing on the art of the possible you will be seen to be positive and you will handle crises well.

19 **Take control**. Influencers do not rely on fate. The IPM agenda (idea, people and money) is a simple way of working towards control. Have a clear idea or plan; enlist the support of the right people and find the money to back your idea and team. With that, you will be in control.

20 **Be persistent**. Believe in yourself. Being rejected and ignored is normal, and makes your final success all the sweeter. The difference between failure and success is often no more than persistence. Never, never give up.

As with any craftsman, the idea is not to use all the tools in your toolkit all at the same time. You need a set of tools you can rely on for different situations. In practice, I will turn to just one or two of the tools above in any situation. Often, that is all you need to turn an awkward situation into a success.

You decide what short cuts and tools you want to use. The important thing is to have something: any method is better than no method. If you have a method and it does not work, at least that gives you the chance to improve your method and move on.

> any method is better than no method

Just as we learn positive short cuts, so we learn from hard experience how to mess up. I have probably earned several gold medals in messing up influencing situations. Fortunately, I have a few tried and trusted methods of messing up. This is fortunate, because if I can avoid these pitfalls I give myself a good chance of succeeding. And although the classic pitfalls are very obvious, they are very easy to fall into. The three big pitfalls are:

1   Falling in love with myself and my idea. The inevitable result is that I talk at people too much and they get bored, annoyed and switch off. That spells F for fail.

2   Not planning properly, and then being surprised by what happens. The biggest planning failure is normally failing to understand how the world looks through the eyes of the other person. That always leads to surprises, which are rarely good. When surprises happen you depend on good fortune to move forward. Influencers should not rely on luck.

3   No options. This is where I am so confident about my own idea and plan, that I fail to plan for any setbacks and have no Plan B. When I depend on one person and one idea and there is a setback, I find myself cornered with no way out. Not good.

Flattery

How many people think that they are below average in terms of honesty, ability, driving, loving, parenting, work, diligence or any other basic human attribute? 95% think they are above average: this is emotionally inevitable and statistically impossible.

How many people think that they are overpaid, over-promoted and over-recognised? Again, virtually no one will admit to such heresy.

We have high regard for ourselves, and suspect that the world fails to recognise the full extent of our innate brilliance, humanity and effort. And then someone comes along who seems to recognise the full extent of our talents. We will naturally form a pretty favourable impression of someone with such good judgement that they see our full worth. We will have just fallen for flattery.

As an influencer you can't do much about people feeling under-promoted and under-paid. But you can do a huge amount to flatter them and make them feel recognised. Here are ten easy ways to flatter:

1   **Give praise**. Be direct, be specific and make it personal.
   - 'The way you handled that client was great – I will try that myself next time'
   - 'Fixing that problem has really helped me'
2   **Ask for advice**. Being asked for advice is flattery because it recognises someone as having insight, skill and capability which you value. It's especially valuable as a way of flattering important people.
3   **Use contradiction** to help make your flattery even more credible.
   - 'I had my doubts about your idea at first – but now I see it could be just what we need!'
4   **Look for the positive**. Even in the most appalling presentation, the presenter will have done something well or said something relevant. Focus on the one relevant and useful thing that was said and show how useful that was. See the deflated presenter reinflate with pride. And even the worst idea will have some good element which you can focus on. Find the silver lining to the cloud.
5   **Ask the flattery question**: 'How on earth did you manage to do that?!'
6   **Praise ten times as much as you criticise, and keep count**. People will want to work with you, because you present no threat, only upside, to their reputation. And if you really have to criticise, it will make more of a mark for being so unusual.
7   **Praise in public and behind people's back**. If private praise is a soft drug, public praise is a hard drug and is totally addictive. So hook them: they will come back for more.
8   **Go for it**. Have your stock of power words that you are comfortable using: brilliant, great, outstanding, top class, best, fantastic. There is no point at which flattery becomes counter-productive, so go all the way.
9   **Be generous**. Do not hog the credit for an idea or action. Share the praise and the glory. This adds to your glory: it makes you look magnanimous and it implies that you are the leader, not the follower. Only the leader is in a position to know how the praise should be shared.
10 **Praise everyone**. Do not have favourites: that is divisive.

It really does not hurt being nice to people. What goes around, comes around: you support other people and they may support you.

Learning the arts of influence and persuasion

Here is a simple test I do whenever I am working with large groups. I ask them how they learn management, leadership or influencing skills. I let them pick two sources of learning from six possibilities. See which two you choose. Do you learn most of your skills from:

- books
- courses
- peers (inside and outside work)
- bosses (positive and negative lessons)
- role models (inside and outside work)
- experience.

Virtually no one chooses books or courses. A forest of hands are raised when it comes to learning from experience. That could be bad news for anyone who writes books and leads courses. But it makes sense. We trust what we have experienced much more than theory in a book or a course. But there is a problem with relying on experience. It turns our learning journey into a random walk: we bump into good experiences and we accelerate our learning. We find ourselves in a bad experience and we quickly go nowhere.

So the purpose of this book, any book, is not to transform you suddenly into a brilliant influencer, persuader, manager or leader. That is not how the world works. Instead, this book will help you remove some of the randomness from the walk of experience. It gives you a structure through which you can make sense of the nonsense you encounter. This lets you accelerate your progress. I took 15 years of trial and error to find out what works and what does not work. This book condenses that experience: you can avoid some of the painful bear traps and develop some of the tools which work. This book is not a substitute for learning or experience: it is a support for your journey.

Starting any journey can seem daunting. The important thing is to start. And then keep going. A simple first step is to try one skill: don't try to master all the skills all at once. Don't worry if it does not work perfectly first time around. Keep working at it, until you find how it works for you and soon enough it will become a natural instinct. Build the skill set one skill at a time. You will find yourself becoming more influential and more persuasive all the time. Your colleagues will not understand how you are achieving such influence, because the skills are invisible to outsiders. You do not work to a script or apply some rigid method: you continue to be who you are and you deploy the new skills in your own unique way.

As with any journey there will be good moments and tough moments. Sometimes you will be on the high road; other times you will find yourself deviating onto exotic byroads. To keep going, you will need to stay focused on your goals. You will also need persistence. And remember that we only excel at what we enjoy. So whatever your journey is, enjoy it.

Index

acting the part 63–77
  looking the part 66–8
  speaking the part 68–71
active listening 31–40
  see also listening
advertising 54, 55, 141
advice, asking 22, 26, 143–5, 233
agenda
aligning 48
  others' view of 133
  own, in meetings 215
agenda control 167, 177–80
agreement 22, 23
  collective 94
  public 23, 81, 83, 93–4,
    161–2, 213
alignment stage 6, 7, 12–13, 230
  traffic lights 24
alliances xvi
  with power barons 168, 170
ambition xiv–xv, 197, 228
  being unreasonable 197–8
  as strategy 196–7
anecdotes, competitive 39, 40
annual appraisals 49, 115
appearance 63
archetypes, ten common 116–20
arguments

begetting arguments 21, 26, 230
  defusing 21–22
  depersonalising 21
  keeping private 81, 83, 93–4,
    159–61
assignments 203, 204–7, 221
  playing hardball 205–6
  tests for right 204–7
attention on speaker 35, 72–3

bankers/banking 68, 104–5,
    144–5, 161
battles 221–2
  avoiding 81, 84
  worth fighting 221
belonging and meaning 149–52
betraying trust 225–6
Blair, Tony 45
body language 34–5
  mirroring 34, 72
  and traffic lights 25
bribery 5, 101
budget negotiations
    203, 211–15, 221
  anchoring 212
  emotional credibility 214
  endorsement 213–14
  framing 213

budget negotiations (*continued*)
  influencing decisions 212–15
  loss aversion 213
  repetition 214–15
  restricted choice 214
  size the prize 215
  strike early 212
Buffet, Warren 207

CEOs: home country bias
    46, 172–3
choices, offering three 19
civil servants case study 92–3
claim to fame 167, 175–7,
    180, 194–5
clients: designing solution 19–20
closed questions 13–14, 33, 39
closing 22–4
coach 190
colleagues, understanding 125–32
  personality tests 125–7
  style compass 127–32
commitment, building xvi–xvii,
    5, 15, 137–63
  building a tribe 138, 149–54
  give to take 100–8
  giving control 138, 154–7
  the hook 138, 139–45
  incremental 137, 184–5, 188,
    192, 229
  IPM method 184–5
  mutual commitment 145–8
  perceived 48–9
  private argument 93–4, 138,
    159–61
  public agreement 93–4, 138,
    157–9, 161–2

  reciprocity xvii, 137–8
  territory principle 148–9
  top three errors 137–8
commitment culture 155–6
commitment mindset xvi–xvii
common interests 34–5, 47
common sense 180
compliance culture 154, 155
concessions 93
  and returns 81, 83
conflict xviii, 203, 220–2
  internal competition 220–1
  keeping private 159–61, 213
  see also battles
conformity 46, 58–9
  dress code 67
  mirroring 67–8
contradiction 36–8, 39, 230
  depersonalising 37–8
  and flattery 233
control xv, xvi 154, 231
  giving 138, 154–7
  through self-control 155–6
corporate entertaining 148–9
creativity 95
credibility 48–51, 230
  borrowing 167–71, 188
  and promises 48–9
  vs. popularity 49–50
crises xviii, 196, 231
creating 51–2
  denial and blame 195, 196
  as opportunities 194–6
criticism 154
cynics 190

deceit 5, 16
decision maker, talking to 26
defensive, becoming 26
difficult conversations 49–50
disclosure 38–9, 230
  competitive 39, 40
distance
  between backgrounds 58–9
  between interests 58
  between saying and hearing 57–8
  four types 54
  and trust 45, 54–9
diversity and conformity 58–9
Dogon 157–8
dress codes 66–8, 150
  aspiration 67, 68
  conservatism 67, 68
  dressing for success 63
  mirroring and conformity 67–8
dumb questions 13–14

emotional aspects 20, 24–5, 230
emotional risk 91, 230
  objections 17, 53, 54
  WIFM 16–17
emotional engagement principle 8
emotional purchases 91–2
empathy, showing 35, 72, 120
  see also walking in others' shoes
endorsement 168, 213–14
engaging people 72–3, 74
enthusiasm 9, 65–6, 74, 77
etiquette 67
expectations, managing 49, 50–1
  in new role 210
eye contact 35, 72

fears 16, 17
  emotional 18
  of rejection 187
fights 221–2
  winning without 81, 84
first impressions 63, 73–4
  generosity 107
first meeting 73
  alignment 12
  building credibility 50
  mutual commitment 146–7
flattery 115, 229
  asking for advice 143–4
  ten ways to flatter 232–3
flexibility xviii
follow up 26
friendship, mask of 8
friendship myth 226
funding 191–3
  size the prize 192, 215
funnelling discussion 8

gatekeepers 190
Gates, Bill 175
generosity 99
  customised 101, 102–4
  earned 101, 104–6
  influential 99, 100–8
  measured 101, 106–7
  as popularity 99–100
  requested not unrequested 108
  ritual and generic 102–3
  saying 'no' gracefully 107
  sharing credit 233
global firms: home country bias
          173–4
goals xvii, xviii, 198

Gono, Gideon 114
gossip 133
grace 70–1
Graham, Billy 71

hearing: rule of five 57–8
homework 11, 26, 87
   for networking 76
hook and commitment
      138, 139–45
   asking for advice 143–5
hook letter 141–3
   personal introductions
      139–40, 142
   teaser 140–3
HR department 204, 207
human nature 230

IBM 175
idea 185–8
   benefits of 15–16
   borrowing credibility 188
   emotional commitment 20
   finding flaws in 187
   outlining proposal 18–20
   PASSION principle 6, 7, 18–20
   talking about 186–7
   traffic lights 25
   ways of generating 185–6
influence vs. persuasion xi–xiii,
      138, 163, 190
informal power 208
information, remembering 35
initiation rites 157–8
interests
   discovering others' 87
   distance between 58
   not positions 81, 83, 84–8, 229

invisibility of influence
      5, 27, 227, 235
IPM: Idea, People, Money 184–94
   and control 231
   finding funding 191–3
idea 185–8
   Plan B 190, 193–4
   support from people
      188–91, 196
   taking over new role 208–11

Japan 161, 172
jargon 56, 57, 70

Kevin Bacon game 139–40
Khanemann, Daniel 212
King, Martin Luther 69

language 48
   and budget negotiations 213
   misleading words 55–7
   power words 233
learning art of influence 234–5
listening 26, 31–40, 71
   active xvi, 31–40
   body language 34–5
   closed questions 33, 39
   common mistakes 39
   contradiction 36–8, 39, 230
   disclosure 38–9, 230
   discovering self–image 120
   letting people talk 8
   open questions 32–4, 39, 40
   for options to explore 89
   paraphrasing 35–6, 39
   principles of 32–9
   reinforcement 34–5, 39
   in situation review 13

talking over people 39, 40
to generate ideas 186
two ears, one mouth xvi,
    8, 31, 230
Lloyds 168
logical risks 53–4
logistics, preparation stage 11
loss of face 93
loyalty 149, 150
luck 124–5

McDonald, Robert 174
Machiavelli myth 226
McKinsey 106, 150
magic myth 227
management
    by letting go 155–7
    control 154
    unreasonable 197–8
MB/TI (Myers–Briggs Type
    Indicators) 125–7
meetings xviii, 203, 215–17
    debriefing 216
    having ideas in 159–60
    informal conversations 217
    own agenda 215
    paraphrasing 36
    speaking in 69, 70–1
    where to look 72–3
meishi (business cards) 13, 172
mentoring relationship 103–4
    patronage 170–1
Microsoft 140, 175
mindset of influence xiv–xviii
mirroring 34, 72
mistakes, classic 26–7
moments of truth 203–22
money as motivator 121

morality myth 227
MPs, British 123
myths of influence 226–7

negotiation
    crafting a story 81, 83, 90–3
    give and take 81, 83
    interests not positions 81, 83,
        84–8
    offering options 81, 83, 87–90
    private argument 81, 83, 93–4
    public agreement 81, 83, 93–4
    soup story 82–3
nemawashi 161
networking 73, 74–6
    introducing yourself 75–6
    steps of 76
new role, taking over 203, 208–11
    budget 210–11
    reorganising team 209–10
    vision as story 208–9
next steps 6, 7, 9, 22–4, 25
    leaving without 26
noddy principle 8, 21, 230

objections
    asking for advice 26
    defusing 21–2
    emotional 17, 53, 54
overcoming 6, 7, 20–2, 25
    PASSION principle 6, 7
off-road vehicles 158–9
open questions 13–14, 32–4, 40
options 8, 229
    failure to have 232
    offering 81, 83, 87–90
Orwell, George 55, 145
outcome focus xvii, 228

P&G 153, 174
pace, space and grace 68–71
Papua New Guinea 66–7
paraphrasing 35–6, 39, 71, 230
partnership principle 8–9, 229
PASSION principle 6–7, 187, 197
   stages 9–24, 192
patronage 168, 169–71
peer group pressure 152
people: right team 188–91
perception management 63
persistence 231
personal assistants 74
personality tests 125–7
persuasion
   dark arts 5
   ten principles of 8–9
   vs. influence xi–xiii, 137, 138,
      163, 190
persuasion judo 20–2
persuasive conversation 5–27
   agree nature of problem 15
   alignment stage 12–13, 24
   classic mistakes 26–7
   closing 22–4
   contradiction 36–8
   disclosure 38–9
   emotional flow 24–5
   focus on their issue 13
   follow up 26
   idea stage 18–20, 25
   invisibility of 5, 27
   next steps 22–4, 25
   overcoming objections 20–2, 25
   PASSION stages 10–24, 27
   preparation stage 10–11, 24
   problems, pre-empting 20
   publicising agreement 23
   reframing problem 14
   reinforcement 34–5
   situation review 13–15, 24
   structure 5, 6–7, 9–24
   traffic lights 24–5
   WIFM stage 15–18, 25
Peters, Tom 175
pitfalls, classic 231–2
Plan B 8, 10, 26–7, 190,
     193–4, 232
planning 230
   failures 232
platform, building 167–80
   agenda control 167, 177–80
   borrowing influence 167–71, 180
   claim to fame 167, 175–7, 180
   employer, choice of 172–4
   endorsement 168
   function, choice of 174–5
   influential people 167–71, 180
   influential places 167, 180
   organisation as power source 172
   patronage 168, 169–71
political benefits 16
politicians 54, 58, 68, 93–4, 100
   Blair 45
   MPs 123
   trust in 44
popularity xvii, 49–50, 100
   weakness from 49, 108, 226, 230
positivity 9, 228, 233
power, informal 208
power sources
   employer 172–3
   endorsement 168
   function 174–5
   organisation 172
   patronage 168, 169–71

power words 233
PowerPoint 27, 219
praise 147, 153, 154, 233
   more than criticise 233
   private and public 233
preparation stage 6, 7, 10–11
   traffic lights 24
presentations 203, 217–20
   questions to ask xviii
   style of presenter 217–18
   success checklist 218–20
   three Es 218
pressure vs. stress 198
price–value discussions 89–90
private, argue in 81, 83, 93–4, 230
private discussions 54, 94
problems as opportunities 194–6
professions, trust in 44
project logic 20
promises 48–9, 50–1
promotion negotiations 84–5, 90
public agreement 81, 83,
       93–4, 230

Queen's questions 32
questions
   closed 33
   open 32–3
   risk/benefits 33–4

rapport building 31, 76, 229
   by paraphrasing 36
reinforcement 35
rational risk 90–1, 230
reciprocity 83, 137
recognition 121, 122, 152–4
   public and private 153
recruitment 73–4

Red Arrows 216
reinforcement 34–5, 39
rejection, fear of 187
repetition 57–8
research in preparation stage 12
respect xvii, 47–8, 49, 120, 230
risk 45, 53–4, 90–1, 230
   emotional 91, 230
   putting benefits first 33–4
   raising 51–2
   removing 230
rules, unwritten 64–5, 77

scripts 113–25
   archetypes 116–20
   changing life chances 124
   dark/bright side 123–4
   influencing using 121–2
   our own 124–5
   partnership 148
   personal 114–16, 121–4, 132
   territorial 148
self-image 121, 144
   understanding people's 115–16,
      132–3
Semler, Ricardo 156
short cuts, twenty 228–31
situation review 6, 7, 13–15
   traffic lights 24
six degrees of separation 139–40
skills of influencing 234–5
smart questions 13–14, 16, 17,
     26, 89
smart/dumb comments 13–14
speaking 68–71
   in meetings 69, 70–1
   pace, space and grace 69–71

sponsor 189, 190
start ups 139, 140
    finding funding 191–2
    looking bigger 73
    Teach First 105–6
    unsuccessful 185
stories, crafting 90–3
stress vs. pressure xv, 198
stretching people xv
strike early 212, 229
style compass 127–32
success
    and acting the part 64, 77
    IPM method 184–94
    obstacles to 183–4
    three Es 65, 77
summarising 71
Sun Tsu: *The Art of War* 221
superiority syndrome 114–15, 232

talking too much 232
Teach First 105–6, 124, 188,
        192–3
    sense of belonging 150–1
technical buyers 189–90
territory principle 148–9
time, generosity with 109
Timpson, John 154
TQM (total quality management)
        155–6
traffic lights 9, 15, 24–5
tribe 32, 77, 138, 149–54
trust xvii, 5, 31, 43–59
    breaking 225–6
    building 108, 230
    degrees of 44
    and distance 45, 54–9
    invisibility of 59

in professions 44
    and risk 45, 51–4
trust equation 45, 59
    values alignment 45, 46–8, 51

unwritten rules 64–5, 77

values 47–8, 51, 191
values alignment 45, 46–8
    conformity vs. diversity 46,
        58–9
venture capitalists 188
Vidal, Marc 140

walking in others' shoes xv–xvi, 8,
        12, 132
weasel words 48–9, 57
WIFM (What's In it For Me) 6,
        7, 15–18
    emotional benefits 16–17
    objections 17
    rational benefits 15–16
    traffic lights 25
win–lose positions 87, 88–9, 95
win–win 8, 229
win–win–win 81–95
    five strands of 81
    mindset 95
Wiseman, Richard 124–5
words
    12 misleading 55–7
    power 233
    weasel 48–9, 57
wrong, being collectively 18, 213
WWF (what we find) concept 26

Zidane, Zinedine 123–4
Zimbabwe 113–14